Lives in Cricket: No 4

John Jackson

The Nottinghamshire Foghorn

Gerald Hudd

First published in Great Britain by
Association of Cricket Statisticians and Historians
Cardiff CF11 9XR.

British Library Cataloguing-in-Publication Data.
A catalogue record for this book is available from the British Library.

ISBN: 978-1-908165-70-1
Typeset and printed by The City Press Leeds Ltd

Contents

Introduction

John Jackson was buried at Toxteth Cemetery in Liverpool in 1901. It was not until 2009 that a headstone was erected over the grave. The story appeared in the *Liverpool Daily Post* which is where I read about it and where my interest in writing a book about Jackson's life and times originated. I have found it a fascinating journey and I can only hope that I have done justice to this cricketer whose wonderful achievements as a player should never be forgotten.

Away from the cricket field John Jackson's personal life has been something of a mystery to unravel. As he died over 110 years ago at a time when genealogy was not such a popular subject as it is now, the answers to some of the mysteries have been lost in the mists of time. This account of his life has therefore been the subject of some conjecture on my part. He led a fascinating life in which he was, in his pomp, the finest fast bowler in the world and the mysteries of his birth and his sad and lonely death should not be allowed to obscure his achievements as a very fine cricketer.

Gerald Hudd
Fearnhead
March 2016

Chapter One
Jackson's Birth and Early Life

It is generally agreed that John Jackson was born on 21st May 1833 at the Suffolk town of Bungay. I say 'generally', because when John Jackson died in Liverpool in November 1901, the death certificate issued by the local coroner gave his age as 74 which would suggest that he was born in 1827. Census returns throw little light on the matter. In the 1871 census his age is recorded as 36 which would make his date of birth sometime in 1835; in 1881 he was shown as being 45 years old suggesting a birthday in 1836. By 1891 he had aged another 13 years in a ten year period and was 58 which agrees with his 1833 date of birth. The records of the Brownlow Hill workhouse in Liverpool, where Jackson was to spend much of his final years and in whose infirmary his death occurred, do not help very much as they record Jackson's age on committal as being between 68 and 72, thus adding to the confusion. I am not at all sure that Jackson was very clear at any stage how old he actually was or where he was born. He always insisted that he was a Nottinghamshire man, born in the Ollerton district of Nottingham.

John Jackson's parentage is another, so far, unresolved mystery. It has not been possible to trace a birth certificate for Jackson. His marriage certificate in 1857 gives his father's name as John, with the occupation of 'hatter'. His mother was undoubtedly one Margaret Jackson, a gypsy lady born in Ireland, who continued to live with her son until her death in Liverpool in the 1870s. But rumours persist, so far unsubstantiated, that Jackson was the 'love child' of an English lord and a gypsy. The link has not been proven, but what is certain, and may well be significant, is that John and his family were rehoused at Wellow in Nottinghamshire within a week of his birth. Wellow was near Rufford Abbey and was part of Lord Savile's estate. The cricketer himself often hinted that he had noble blood in his veins. It may have been thought politic to move the child to another part of the country before any similarities between his features and those of one of the local noblemen became too apparent.

It might well have been that there was some sort of private income to tide the family over until Jackson's cricket career took off. The census returns of 1841 and 1851 are of no help as neither Jackson nor his mother appear on either. It is all conjecture, but it might explain how the Jackson family survived on little income.

Jackson's parents were both gypsies well used to the travelling life, a fact that John may have inherited which would have been useful to him in the role of an itinerant cricketer. He was an only child. The little family lived in humble circumstances in a cottage in Wellow with little prospect of aspiring to anything better. Whatever schooling the young John Jackson received was rudimentary which may account for the age discrepancies on the census returns. Apart from struggling with his figure work he was unable to sign his own name on his son Harry's birth certificate in 1865 and had to resort to the illiterate's 'mark' in the space for the father's signature. What would have become of him had he not been good at the game of cricket is beyond imagining. We should not, however, be too surprised at this lack of a formal education. With the industrial revolution in full swing in England in the 1830s, very few children received any sort of education apart from those whose parents could afford to send them to be educated at a public school. Indeed, compared to the lot of many children who were forced to spend long hours working in the mills in northern England, Jackson was fairly lucky to be able to hone his cricket skills on the village green and occasionally work for the local farmers.

Wellow is a village in the Nottinghamshire district of Ollerton. It has a village green upon which young John Jackson played his first cricket. He learnt how to bowl straight by bowling at milestones on the highway. He grew into a big, strong boy with the ideal build for hurling down the thunderbolt deliveries which were to make him famous. Besides practising his cricket, he strengthened his legs and improved his stamina by following the hunt in the Rufford country during the winter months. The Rufford amalgamated with the Grove in 1957 and is now known as the Grove and Rufford Hunt.

Jackson's childhood home was situated in what was then a hotbed of Nottinghamshire cricket with powerful clubs like Newark and Southwell lying within a comfortable radius of Wellow. The future All-England cricketer became one of the crack bowlers on the village green at Wellow where he spent all his time practising his cricket when he was not doing odd jobs for the local farmers. As he grew bigger and stronger he took to walking the seven miles to Southwell each day where he would hang about the cricket ground watching the club cricketers practise until someone threw him a sixpence to 'send a few down' at them. It did not take these experienced players long to realise that they had discovered a potential diamond.

Cricket had been played at Southwell since the 18th century. The earliest reference to a match there dates back to 6th September 1787. Lord Byron was known to have practised there wearing any number of waistcoats to sweat some weight off and to keep fit. When the young Jackson first walked into the ground, the club's star players were the Tinley brothers - Francis Edward, Robert Crispin and Vincent - all of whom played for Nottinghamshire, with R.C.Tinley achieving everlasting fame as a lob bowler. In his early days R.C. had been a fast bowler, but later in his career he adopted a slow under-arm delivery which proved the perfect contrast to the pace and hostility of Jackson at the other end. The pair were to provide fearful opposition to inexperienced local batsmen in the odds matches played by the All-England Eleven. The Tinleys were instrumental in introducing Jackson to William Clarke and the All-England Eleven and thence to the Nottinghamshire County Cricket Club.

Jackson is believed to have first played for Southwell as a professional cricketer in the 1850 season although early records are sparse and the first mention of his name on a scorecard comes when he made an appearance for Twenty-Two of Newark against an All-England Eleven in a three-day match beginning on 5th August 1852.

It is instructive to look at how cricket was played when Jackson was playing. The first thing to note is the generally poor quality of the grounds on which the game was played. Even at a ground like Lord's the main instrument for keeping the grass cropped consisted of a flock of sheep which were kept in a pen in one corner of the ground. Pebbles were often found on pitches. As late as 1870 George Summers died after being struck on the head by a delivery which lifted sharply off a dodgy pitch. It was possible for good players to construct an innings on them. William Ward managed to make 278 for MCC against Norfolk at Lord's in 1820 – a ground record that stood until 1925 when Percy Holmes made 315, but conditions were much worse on many of the grounds on which the All-England Eleven had to play where it was often impossible to distinguish the pitch from the rest of the field which made batting a hazardous pursuit, especially when a bowler of Jackson's pace was performing.

Bowling was mainly round-arm which had been legalised in 1835 although under-arm bowling was still lawful and William Clarke himself continued to take many wickets with slow right-arm leg-spin bowling and mighty effective he was too. Round-arm meant that the ball had to be delivered with the hand somewhere between waist and shoulder-height. This was to remain the legitimate delivery until 1864 although notable players, such as W.G.Grace, continued with round-arm after that.

Overs were of four balls and the bowler could only change ends once during an innings. Fielding positions were broadly similar to today apart from that of long stop which was then a vital position.

Chapter Two

John Jackson - Cricketer

There is a marvellous description of Jackson's bowling in Volume V of Arthur Haygarth's *Scores and Biographies* which captures the bowler perfectly, and all the other writers - and there are many of them - agree with the description in almost every detail:

> He was one of the straightest, fastest and best bowlers that has ever appeared, and though his speed was so great, he delivered easily to himself, all weathers suiting him. By some he was called 'the demon bowler', and his delivery was unexceptional as to fairness .... His career, though rather short, must be considered most brilliant.

He had the fast bowler's temper too. Any batsman who had the temerity to stand up to him and, even worse, smash him to the boundary, could expect instant retaliation in the form of a fast and vicious beamer coming whistling at the intrepid batsman's head. Jackson had another habit, peculiar to himself. Every time he took a wicket he blew his nose violently. As he took rather a lot of wickets pretty frequently, this adenoidal clearout earned him the nickname of 'Foghorn'. His other nickname was 'Gypsy', a reference to his possible parentage. He was tall, 6ft 1/4 inch, and weighed 14 stone which later expanded to 15.

His great years as a bowler were between 1857 and 1863. His figures are set out in the Appendix, but suffice it to say here that he took 671 wickets in first-class matches in these seasons and that only one century was scored against a side for whom Jackson was playing. The century was hit by William Caffyn of Surrey who has gone on record as saying that he considered Jackson to be a far superior bowler to his other great contemporary speedster, George Tarrant of Cambridgeshire. According to Caffyn, Jackson bowled straighter, kept a better length than Tarrant and was equally as fast. Just for the record nine first-class hundreds were hit by players on Jackson's side in the same set of matches.

A bowler of Jackson's pace on the fiery wickets of the day made life very difficult for batsmen, and this led to Jackson being the subject of the first cricket cartoon to appear in the pages of *Punch* magazine. A much battered cricketer is shown returning from a match and a bystander approaches him:

> Bystander: Good match, old fellow?
> Cricketer: Oh yes, awfully jolly.
> Bystander: What did you do?
> Cricketer: I 'ad a hover of Jackson; the first ball 'it me on the hand,

the second 'ad me on the knee, the third was in me eye and the fourth bowled me out.

CRICKET.—THE PRIDE OF THE VILLAGE.

The Punch cartoon.

Jackson could be a real destroyer against the local Twenty-Twos who comprised the main opposition to the All-England Eleven. His performances will be dealt with in detail later in this book, but just a few of the more outstanding ones can be listed as a 'taster':

1857	25 for 37 runs v Twenty-Two of Uppingham, including six wickets in seven balls.
1857	20 for 30 runs v Twenty of Shropshire at Aston Hall.
1858	16 for 62 runs v Sixteen of Oxford University.
1858	24 for 61 runs v Twenty-Two of Monmouthshire.
1859	10 for 1 run v Twenty-Two of Cornwall at Redruth.
1861	26 for 44 runs v Twenty-Two of Derbyshire at Chesterfield.
1862	17 for 63 runs v Sixteen of Oxford University.

Many of his victims were probably taken before the nervous batsman had arrived at the crease. There is a famous story of the batsman who gave himself out rather than face another of the bowler's thunderbolts, even though the umpire had not given him out and the bowler had not even appealed. Such was the terror that this man produced among local batsmen unused to facing bowling of such velocity.

Jackson's main strength was his bowling, fast, straight and round arm, but there were other facets to his game which he developed further as his career blossomed. He became a hard-hitting batsman whose powerful build and long reach proved invaluable to him. He had one first-class century to his credit, made for Nottinghamshire v Kent at Cranbrook in 1863, and he also hit scores of 59 against Surrey at Kennington Oval in 1862, 52 against Yorkshire at Bradford in 1864 and 55 against Yorkshire at Trent Bridge in 1865. He made an unbeaten 68 for England against a Kent XIII in 1864, and 55 for the All-England Eleven against XVIII of Manchester Broughton Club in 1865. As a fieldsman he generally fielded at short slip but later stood in the long field. He had a safe pair of hands and took 117 catches in important matches.

When John Jackson's star began to light up the cricket firmament, cricket had not yet become the universal game which exists today. Matches subsequently given first-class status were few and far between. In 1854 there were 29 such games which gradually increased to 51 in 1870. Public school cricket began to get underway in the 1850s and 1860s. Of the wandering clubs, I Zingari was founded in 1845, Gentlemen of Worcestershire in 1848, Quidnuncs in 1851, Harlequins in 1856, and Free Foresters in 1856. It would appear from what research has been carried out so far that plenty of cricket was being played but at a local level.

Other developments were the first Lancashire v Yorkshire match in 1849, the opening of the Bramall Lane ground in Sheffield in 1855. The Cricketers Fund Friendly Society was set up in 1857 to provide some financial support for former professionals who had fallen on hard times. 1862 saw the appearance of Arthur Haygarth's first volume of *Scores and Biographies*, John Wisden published his first Almanack in 1864 followed by *John Lillywhite's Cricketers' Companion* in 1865. The first overseas tours were made to the USA and Canada in1859 and then Australia and New Zealand in 1861/62.

Probably the most significant cricketing development in the mid-nineteenth century and one which was central to Jackson's career, however, was the formation of William Clarke's All-England Eleven.

Chapter Three

The All-England Eleven

The All-England Eleven was formed in 1846 by William Clarke, a Nottinghamshire bricklayer, who conceived the idea as a means of capitalising on the growing public interest in cricket that was arising in the mid-19th century. The objective was to draw together a team of the best professional players from around the country to form an itinerant eleven which would travel the length and breadth of England, playing odds matches against local teams who were often 'beefed up' by professionals to make the encounters more even. Clarke charged admission to these matches, taking charge of the gate receipts himself and paying his men on a sliding scale according to their performances in each match.

There is no doubt that the greatest beneficiary of this system was Clarke himself whose parsimony was legendary, and in 1852 a number of professionals, fed up with Clarke's dictatorial manner, formed a breakaway team which they called the United All-England Eleven. Henceforth there would be two itinerant elevens touring the country as well as playing each other, although the All England Eleven v the United All England Eleven matches did not start until after Clarke's death.

The All-England Eleven continued to tour the country until 1879 whereas the United All England Eleven lasted until 1869 and further splits between the players saw the formation of the United North of England Eleven, which played between 1870 and 1881, and the United South of England Eleven which lasted from 1870 to 1882.

Apart from Clarke's dictatorial manner, tightness with money and what we would call a lack of 'man- management' skills, there were other reasons for the formation of the United All-England Eleven. There were so many local Twenty-Twos wanting to test their skills against the best professional players in the land that it would have been impossible for one eleven to fit in all the fixtures even if they played two matches every week between April and October. Clarke had also recruited so many professionals into his troupe that he could not keep them all occupied, so it is highly likely that a split would have occurred even if Clarke had got along with everybody.

The professional elevens travelled vast distances. Consider this itinerary for the All-England Eleven in 1856. All the matches were of three days duration.

15 May	Oxford at Christchurch Ground, Oxford
19 May	Durham
2 June	South Wales at Neath
5 June	Cirencester at Cirencester Park

12 June	Downham Market
16 June	Whitehaven
19 June	Manchester Broughton Club at Salford
23 June	Enville Hall, Stamford, Lincolnshire
26 June	Trowbridge, Wiltshire
14 July	Melton Mowbray
17 July	Sleaford, Lincolnshire
24 July	Maidstone, Kent
4 August	Nottingham Commercial Club at Trent Bridge
14 August	Bristol
18 August	Stoke-on-Trent
21 August	Nottinghamshire at Trent Bridge
25 August	Newark-on-Trent
29 August	Hull
22 September	Stockton-on-Tees
25 September	Leeds

When you consider that rail travel, although expanding, was still in its infancy and did not reach to all parts of the country and that travel by train was nowhere near the comfortable and speedy way to travel that it is today, it is remarkable to think that teams should contemplate such an itinerary.

The expansion of the railway network was a major factor in the mid-nineteenth century expansion of cricket. Following on from the Rainhill Trials of 1829 and the opening of the Liverpool to Manchester railway, a basic network was quickly developed which by 1855 covered most of the country. All this meant that the itinerant elevens were able to reach far-flung parts of the country far more easily.

Prior to this travel between major destinations had been by stage coach or the canal network. The railway was faster than these and enabled cricketers to finish a match one evening and start another one the following morning. This all speeded up the further expansion of county cricket and later the start of international cricket.

Richard Daft, a member of the All-England Eleven, has left us a wonderful description of a journey made in 1859 by the Eleven to fulfil a fixture at Redruth in Cornwall, probably just before the completion of the line from Plymouth to Penzance. Travelling along, by coach, on a wild and deserted road with a deep ditch on either side, their problems increased when they ran into a violent thunderstorm. Playing for the team on this occasion was one, Captain Handley, a veteran of the Crimean War, who had charged fearlessly into the Russian guns at Balaclava as a member of the Light Brigade. The good Captain confirmed later that the violence of this storm frightened him more than the Russian guns and he let fly some choice and lurid remarks about the weather, the road and the team's general situation. The Captain's profane language added to the nervousness of the All-England captain, George Parr of Nottinghamshire, and he asked Handley to moderate his language, fearful that he would bring down the wrath of the heavens upon the whole team.

At length the coach arrived at an isolated cottage where the team hoped to be able to obtain some food and temporary shelter. Their cries and knocking produced no response for a time; then suddenly an old man in a nightcap appeared at an upper window clutching an old blunderbuss pointed straight at Parr's head. This did nothing to soothe the nerves of the AEE captain, but the team managed to calm the old fellow down although the process took some time as he was as deaf as a post. Finally, cheese and beer were produced, paid for and swiftly consumed and the team prepared to continue their journey, only to find that one man was missing. This man was their star bowler, John Jackson, who was discovered emerging from the dairy looking like a man covered in shaving lather. The lather turned out to be clotted cream, a large bowl of which Jackson had discovered and got stuck into to such good effect that he had left very little behind for his team-mates to consume.

Another hazard that the team encountered around the cricket fields of England was the poor and rough condition of many of them. Some grounds consisted of a pitch surrounded by long grass reaching to the fieldsmen's shins and, once, in Truro, a deep fielder chasing after a ball put up a whole covey of partridges in the outfield. The poor standard of the pitches on which they had to play undoubtedly played a part in the low-scoring characteristic of many games. Another factor was the difficulty for the Eleven when faced with twenty fielders plus the bowler and wicketkeeper, which rendered run scoring very difficult. Hits mostly had to be 'run out' and only hits out of the ground were counted as six. A batsman playing a long innings covered a lot of ground running up and down the pitch to score his and his partner's runs.

Chapter Four

Early Career, Marriage and Family

We left the John Jackson story at the point at which he began his professional career with the Southwell Cricket Club in 1850. Records of his early matches have, sadly, been lost, and the first game in which his name appears on an official scorecard was the match between the All-England Eleven and Twenty-Two of Newark on 5, 6, and 7 August 1852. In this match Jackson was run out for nought in his only innings but did well with the ball, taking six of the AEE wickets for 49 runs, five of his victims being bowled. With F.Tinley's help he bowled the Eleven out for 106, his wickets including such illustrious names as William Martingell, George Parr, Thomas Box, Nicholas Felix, John Bickley and William Caffyn. He dismissed Parr out in the second innings as well but not before the Nottinghamshire professional had scored 66. He also took the wicket of George Anderson to finish with two for 51. William Clarke was playing in this match for the AEE and he must have noticed with interest the way some of his best players had struggled against this strong and pacy newcomer. The match finished in a draw with the Newark men having scored 49 for four in their second innings chasing 132 to record a famous victory.

Jackson told the local paper that he had been most hospitably entertained and could not refrain from shedding a few tears. The paper noted that when he bowled Thomas Box, two of the stumps were knocked out of the ground. It does not mention whether Box was upset about this!

Jackson's next appearance for which a record remains was for Twenty-Two of Spalding against the AEE on 4, 5, 6, August 1853, an exciting match which the Spalding team won by just one run. Jackson made 11(top score in an innings of 57) and 2 with the bat and took three for 18 and five for 27 with the ball. He also took a catch. Amongst his victims in the second innings was the legendary Alfred Mynn, the old lion of Kent, who was caught by G.Armitage for 20. A possible second appearance by Jackson in the 1853 season was the game at Ipswich between the AEE and XIX of Ipswich in which a player named Jackson appears for Ipswich as one of their 'given' professionals. This may have been John Jackson or possibly William Jackson, another Nottinghamshire professional who was a contemporary player. The only indication that may be relevant is that the Jackson who played took eight wickets, a regular feat for John but not so for William.

We lose sight of Jackson in 1854 when he was believed to be fulfilling a professional engagement with the Grange Club in Edinburgh, so our next confirmed sight of him is in the 1855 season when he played for Twenty-

Two of Newark against the AEE on 26, 27, 28, July in a match got up by the Mayor of Newark, Mr W.Ragsdale, who was a generous and liberal supporter of the game. Newark won the match by 49 runs, helped by Jackson taking seven wickets for 11 runs in the AEE second innings. This match was typical of the low scoring matches of the era. E.Willsher took twelve wickets for 14 runs in the Newark second innings of 37 all out in which twelve wickets in succession fell without any addition to the score. The AEE was then bowled out, mostly by Jackson, for 35 runs which meant that thirty-one wickets had fallen for just 72 runs.

Jackson's next match took place at the racecourse ground at Stamford where he played as a 'given' man for a Stamford and District Twenty-Two against the AEE in a match which began on 30 July and ended in a draw. Brass bands were in attendance to entertain spectators during breaks in play and around the ground there were numerous tents and marquees surmounted with flags. The Mayor of Stamford presided at a dinner for 100 which took place at 3.00 pm on the second day, play being badly interrupted by rain. In the play that was possible Jackson made a fine contribution scoring 37 (top score) in Stamford's first innings and 18 (run out) in the second. With the ball he captured five AEE wickets for 72 runs.

It is clear from the fact that Jackson played as a given man at Stamford that he was now beginning to develop a reputation. This is confirmed by his debut for the All-England Eleven which came on 2 August 1855 when he played for the Eleven against Twenty-Two of Spalding, Lincolnshire. The Twenty-Two were outclassed by the professional Eleven and beaten by an innings. Jackson opened the batting for AEE, scoring 6. His bowling was not needed much as Willsher took seventeen wickets for 23 and twelve for 19 in the match. Jackson was only on long enough to take two for 13 in the second innings. The local paper reported the large gathering of ladies who attended the match in their gay attire and waxed lyrical about the flags gently waving in the breeze, the white tents and the natural beauty of the setting. A visit from the AEE was clearly a big event.

On 16 August Jackson made his first-class debut at Trent Bridge, the home of Nottinghamshire cricket in a match between Nottinghamshire and an England XI got up by William Clarke from amongst his All-England players. Over the years Jackson was to play for Nottinghamshire in 37 matches in first-class cricket. He took three wickets for 28 and none for 18, held a catch and scored 8 and 10. A total of 601 runs were scored in the drawn game for the loss of thirty-three wickets. Haygarth complained that no bowling analyses for this match could be found in *Bell's Life* or indeed the AEE scorebook. It is worth noting at this stage that Haygarth's *Scores and Biographies* which I have used as my Bible for Jackson's cricket career contains many references to there being alternative versions to the score given, and that often even the official scorebooks did not agree. It is hard therefore to compile the definitive bowling career for Jackson. Clearly statistics did not mean very much in those early cricketing days.

Jackson's next match was at Dudley on 20 August where he played for the All-England Eleven in an exciting match against Twenty-Two of

Dudley, a game which the AEE won by the narrow margin of 5 runs in a tense finish. This was due in no small measure to Jackson's bowling. Although he scored but 2 and 4 with the bat, his bowling was sufficiently and consistently hostile that he bowled 25.3 (4 ball) overs in the Dudley first innings, taking four wickets for 6 runs, and 30.1 overs in the second innings to take ten for 27 - figures of 14-33 in the match.

Lillywhite's Guide states that John Jackson played for Twenty-Two of Leicestershire against the AEE in a game at Leicester beginning on 23 August, but other sources believed the participant to have been William Jackson. The Jackson who did take part took six for 37 and two for 22 which sounds like a 'Foghorn' performance but we cannot be certain. Writing about the same match *Bell's Life* asserts that a C.Hoskins played rather than the T.Selby who is given as a player in *Scores and Biographies.* The only other evidence I can offer is an interview given by Jackson to A.W.Pullin and published in Pullin's book, *Talks with Old England Cricketers.* Jackson refers to some difficulties one of the umpires had in getting from Leicester to Hereford to take part in the next AEE match. This is the only occasion I can find on which a match at Hereford immediately succeeded one at Leicester. Is this conclusive? Some of the other episodes mentioned by Jackson in his interview do not quite tie in with actual events.

There is no argument about Jackson's next opponents as he played for the AEE against Twenty-Two of Hereford on 27 August, taking two for 19 in the local team's only innings and scoring 0 and 15. The match was drawn very much in favour of the AEE whose second innings score of 281 suggests a better prepared pitch than the ones they normally played on.

The next opposition for the AEE was a game against XVIII of the Nottingham Commercial Club at the Old Forest Ground in Nottingham where William Clarke had first appeared in a great match in 1817. The AEE won this match by four wickets. Jackson's bowling was not used, there being only four double figure scores among the 36 Club batsmen who went to the crease. He batted well scoring 14 and 13. The next game, against Twenty-Two of Leeds, was won by AEE by ten wickets with Jackson taking five for 24 in Leeds' second innings.

Some sources, but not Haygarth, claim that John Jackson appeared as a given man for Twenty-Two of Birmingham against the United All-England Eleven at Small Heath, Birmingham on 10 September. *Scores and Biographies* states that William, not John, played, but figures of six for 24 and seven for 29 in the UAEE innings are suggestive of a John Jackson performance. However, it is hard to find conclusive proof. He certainly did appear for the AEE in their final match of the season at Anlaby Road, Hull on 17 September. He scored 2 and 4 and bowled eight overs in the Hull second innings, taking two for 7. None of the Hull batsmen reached 10 in their first innings, with Clarke (eight wickets) and Willsher (twelve), proving too much for the inexperienced local players. Rain meant the game finished in a draw but did not prevent a large assemblage of ladies and gentlemen from attending each day.

After a winter's rest Jackson was back in action for the summer of 1856. He played regularly throughout the season making appearances in first-class matches, but most of his time was spent with the All-England Eleven

As far as first-class matches are concerned John Jackson made his second appearance for Nottinghamshire on 21 August 1856 at Newark, playing against an England XI that included Alfred Mynn, H.H.Stephenson and the delightfully named Julius Caesar. Jackson took four wickets in a hard-fought match which England won by 7 runs.

He made two appearances in the North and South fixtures, major matches in those days. This included his first ever match at Lord's which took place on 30 June and 1 July and which was won by the South by six wickets. Jackson was run out without scoring in North's first innings of 117 but then blasted out the first three batsmen of the South, W.Nicholson, S.Ponsonby and E.Willsher for 11, 1 and 0 respectively. South were then 22 for four but recovered to make 170 with Jackson's figures being three for 41 in 19 overs, five of them maidens. North made 96 second time around, Jackson scoring 11. Jackson bowled Julius Caesar for 1 but could not prevent South winning the match who took 24.2 overs to make the 44 needed – Jackson taking one for 12.

The return match at the Broughton Club ground in Salford, Manchester was ruined by the weather. North made 219 (Jackson 5) and South were 46 for three when the rain came. Jackson bowled W.Nicholson out for 24 in taking one for 17 in twelve overs.

For All-England matches in 1856 the team' itinerary has already been listed. Jackson played in 19 matches for them of which 11 were won, 5 lost and 3 drawn. He took 166 wickets for 609 runs although the rider has to be added that some of the bowling figures shown in *Scores and Biographies* are not necessarily strictly accurate. Haygarth made the general comment that bowling analyses do not always tally with the number of runs scored off the bat. In the matches he played, Jackson batted 29 times, scoring 90 runs, with five innings being not outs. He took nine catches.

Some highlights of the season (all against Twenty-Twos) were his twenty-one wickets for 58 runs against Stockton, eighteen for 69 against Loughborough, fourteen for 43 against Maidstone, sixteen for 35 against Trowbridge, fifteen for 45 at Loughborough against Stoke-on-Trent and 14 for 40 against Sleaford.

A flavour now of some of the games gleaned from contemporary match reports in local papers. We read of a fine military band entertaining spectators at Durham. There were 33 ducks made in the match against Twenty-Two of South Wales at Neath. No member of the local side passed double figures and 26 of the ducks were made by their batsmen. This match was played under the patronage of the Marquis of Bute. The correspondent of the local paper spent four lengthy paragraphs describing the facilities provided for spectators, without once mentioning the cricket or even giving the result of the match. In a match at Downham Market the first seven wickets of the local Twenty-Two fell without a run being scored.

At Melton Mowbray Jackson guested for the local Twenty-Two and took six AEE wickets. At Sleaford he ran riot, taking fourteen for 40 with only two local men scoring double figures. His 'foghorn' must have been noticeable on that occasion! Maidstone saw him playing against the great Alfred Mynn when he bowled the old master for a duck in his second innings. In a violent overnight storm at Maidstone the refreshment tent was blown down and had to be replaced. In a match against the Nottingham Commercial Club Haygarth mentioned that other accounts credit Jackson with the wicket of J.Marfleet, a wicket that Haygarth's account credited to W.S.Fiennes. Against Twenty-Two of Leeds the last twelve Leeds wickets fell for only 4 runs, but rain which arrived on the last day prevented a finish. In its report of the match at Stoke-on-Trent the *Midland Counties Advertiser* was moved to write about 'Jackson's invincible bowling'. Only two bowlers were used by each side in this match which was an unusual occurrence. Parr, the AEE captain, objected to one of Stoke's given man, Bickley, and offered the locals A.Crossland instead out of his own team, with J.Collins of Stoke playing for the AEE. Stoke got the best of this bargain as Crossland delivered 59 balls in the AEE first innings without a run being scored off him and took five for 11 in the second innings, whilst Collins made two ducks for the AEE. Stoke won the match by 40 runs. Spectators were entertained by a brass band and a pianoforte and concertina. Scoring was very low with four completed innings amounting to no more than 212 runs.

Before we leave 1856 behind we should mention two other games that Jackson participated in during the season. He had been engaged as a professional bowler to coach the students of Cambridge University in the Spring Term and, in this capacity, he joined with other professionals similarly engaged to play a match against a Cambridge University team on 24, 25 and 26 April. He took two wickets in the match for 46 runs but had the misfortune to bag a 'pair' with the bat. The University team won the match by 28 runs. Later in the season he took part in a match at Leamington Spa between the Players and Fifteen Gentlemen of England, scoring 8* and 10, and taking nought for 14 and four for 26 as the Gentlemen won by 43 runs. Jackson's debut in the more prestigious Players v Gentlemen fixture was not to be long delayed.

He had a magnificent season in 1857 taking more than three hundred wickets in all matches. He was often seriously over-bowled, on one occasion at Bradford bowling 101 four-ball overs in the match, but he was the main strike bowler for most of the teams in which he played. He was a prolific wicket taker and a willing and strong worker, so the temptation to bowl him was overwhelming. Such serious over-bowling, though, almost certainly shortened his career and led to the injury which caused his retirement from first-class cricket at the age of only 33. As a batsman he went to the crease on 51 occasions for a highest score of 27, but his fielding was, as usual, excellent and he pouched 29 catches in all games.

A major development in the 1857 fixture list was the beginning of the series of matches between the All-England Eleven and the United England

Eleven. We have seen how the All-England Eleven split up into the AEE and the UAEE, with the AEE being composed primarily of the northern professionals and the UAEE mostly of players from the south.

Whilst William Clarke was still alive he remained an obstacle to any meeting of the two Elevens even though there would have been great public interest in seeing a clash between the leading professional teams of the day. All this changed after Clarke died on 25 August 1856. Early in the following year it was suggested by friends of Jimmy Dean, a founder member of the UAEE and a ground bowler at Lord's who had been playing before the public for twenty years, that he should be granted a benefit match to be played at Lord's between the two great Elevens. A challenge was sent to George Parr, captain of the AEE, who accepted with one stipulation – that some of the proceeds should go to the Cricketers Fund Friendly Society which had been set up to offer help to former cricketers who had fallen upon hard times. Sad to relate, this is exactly what happened to John Jackson in later life. Parr's proposal was accepted and the first match was arranged for Lord's, beginning on Whit Monday, 1 June 1857. It was the start of an epic series of matches.

A crowd estimated at 10,000 was present on the first day, including members of the nobility, and they witnessed John Jackson carry all before him in taking six wickets for 31 in 25.3 overs. He bowled out three of the top five UAEE batsmen, James Dean, William Caffyn and John Wisden. The UAEE total was 143 and the AEE replied with 206, George Parr making 56 and Heathfield Stephenson 51. The lead was 63 and the UAEE were bowled out in their second innings for 140 (Jackson two for 54 off 35 overs). The AEE made the 78 runs they needed for the loss of five wickets.

On 27 July the two teams met again at Lord's, playing this time for the benefit of Jimmy Dean who received the gratifying sum of upwards of £400. In this match Wisden and Caffyn dismissed the AEE for 99 (George Parr 48). The UAEE replied with 126, Jackson taking three for 48 in 45 overs. Steady batting took the AEE to 214 with Diver (46), Parr (36) and R.C.Tinley (46) all making substantial contributions. The UAEE needed 188 to win but collapsed to 54 all out, leaving the AEE winners by 133 runs. The main destroyer for the AEE in this match was Edgar Willsher who took ten wickets in the match. Jackson's part in UAEE's second innings debacle was two for 22 in 28 overs. At a small ceremony held after the AEE match against Richmond, North Yorkshire later in the season, George Parr's fine batting in these two matches in which he had made 56*, 19*, 48 and 36 was honoured by the presentation of a gold watch.

1857 was the year in which Jackson made his first appearance in the famous Lord's fixture, Gentlemen v Players, on 13 and 14 July. It was played in a heat wave and Jackson was, for once, used sparingly, bowling 8.1 overs in the first innings and 9 in the second, and taking the wickets of V.E.Walker and W.Nicholson, both bowled. In a close and interesting game the Players won by 13 runs. For the Gentlemen R.Hankey scored 70 and A.Haygarth 57 in their first innings total of 194 which conceded a lead of 5 runs to the Players. In the second innings the Players were dismissed for 122 which left the Gentlemen needing 128 to win. E.T.Drake made a slashing innings of 58 but their other batsmen failed and in the end the number of extras conceded was decisive. The Gentlemen gave away 40 and the Players 26, a difference of 14 in a match where the margin of victory was only 13.

Jackson played in four other matches for an England XI: two against a combined Kent and Sussex team which were won by England, and two against a combined Surrey and Sussex team both of which England lost. The first match against Kent & Sussex was played at Lord's on 6 and 7 July, with England winning by 13 runs despite being dismissed in 90 minutes by Wisden and Willsher in their second innings. W.Goodhew seemed to be carrying the combined side to victory until Jackson bowled him for 40 in the course of taking three for 20 in 21 overs. England won much more conclusively at Canterbury on 17, 18 and 19 August, winning by 149 runs. Jem Grundy hit scores of 50 and 58, Parr made 73 and H. Stephenson 48 as England totalled 186 and 166. Jackson had a herculean stint of bowling, 36 overs in the first innings and 22 in the second. He took three for 47 and three for 28, as Kent & Sussex made 136 and 67.

In a heat wave at the Kennington Oval on 3, 4 and 5 August Jackson bowled even more heroically. He bowled at one end throughout both the Surrey & Sussex innings (363 deliveries altogether) taking seven for 69 and six for 76, being the sole cutting edge of the England attack with Willsher unable to play. The combined team hit up 151 and 221 (T.Lockyer 62). The England scores were 203, before utterly collapsing in the second innings for 59, Caffyn taking nine for 29. George Parr was the sole batsman to cope, scoring 25 not out. Only three England batsmen were bowled as Surrey/Sussex won by 110 runs.

A week later, at Hove, England were embarrassed again, being bowled out by Wisden and Griffith for a mere 33 and 51. Surrey & Sussex won by an innings and 39 despite scoring no more than 123 themselves. For the third innings in succession Jackson bowled throughout, a total of 38.3 overs in which he took eight wickets for 45. With more bowling support for Jackson the scoring would have been low enough to justify a visit from today's pitch inspectors!

Jackson's other five first-class matches in 1857 were all for the North of England, three of them against the South and the other two against Surrey. In these games he took a further forty-seven wickets. In the match at Kennington Oval on 9 July against Surrey he was made to work hard for his wickets, bowling a total of 53 overs to take four for 84. Caffyn hit 60 for Surrey before Jackson bowled him. Surrey finished on 226 and bowled the North out for 81 and 176, leaving the County side to get 32 to win. They reached 30 for one and then Jackson took three wickets in an over. He had H.H.Stephenson caught off the first ball, bowled F.P.Miller with the second and then bowled G.Griffith with the fourth and last ball of the over. Surrey scrambled the last two runs at the other end to win by six wickets, Jackson finishing with three for 11 off 11 overs.

On 20 July Jackson lined up again for the North against the South at Lord's. In another epic bowling performance he sent down 41 overs to take eight for 53 in the South's first innings of 165, and 32 overs to take seven for 38 in their second innings of 95. Fifteen wickets in an eleven-a-side game was a feat rarely achieved, but his side still lost by 14 runs, making only 124 and 122 in their innings. Caffyn – how that name keeps cropping up – hit 90 in the first innings of the South, and T.Lockyer made 40. Eleven of Jackson's victims were bowled.

Jackson had another fine match for the North against the South at Tunbridge Wells on 13 and 14 August. He took thirteen wickets for 44 in a low-scoring match in which the highest team total was 71. With W. Martingell operating at the other end he once again bowled unchanged in both innings. Set 71, highest score of the match to win, the North got them with surprising ease. A low-scoring match between the North and Surrey at Bramall Lane on 24 and 25 August saw Surrey emerge victorious by five wickets. Caffyn – that man again - and Griffith bowled the North out twice for 73 and 63, helped by five of the North batsmen running themselves out, one of their opening batsmen, T.Hunt, managing to do this in both innings for 0 and 7 respectively. Surrey made 93 and 45 for five with Jackson taking three for 53 in the match from 44 overs.

Jackson's final first-class match of the season on 7, 8 and 9 September at Trent Bridge ended in a draw, with the North scoring 50 and 115 and South replying with 54 and 97 for eight, although with John Wisden hurt and possibly unable to bat, this may be counted as nine. And thereby hangs a tale. John Jackson never took all ten wickets in a first-class match, but in an interview he gave to A.W.Pullin (Old Ebor), included in Pullin's book, *Talks with Old England Cricketers*, he claimed that in a North v South match he once took nine wickets and lamed John Wisden so that he could not complete his innings – 'so that was as good as all ten'. In actual fact it was only nine because one of the batsmen, W.Mortlock, was dismissed by F.Bell, although as he was caught by Jackson we can perhaps stretch a point. Jackson's figures were eight for 20 and in the second innings one for 10.

In 12 first-class matches in 1857 Jackson bowled a mammoth 596.2 overs, 247 maidens and took 92 wickets for 788 runs, an average of 8.56. He took 9 catches. It was truly a magnificent performance.

In addition to all this, John Jackson took part in 15 of the AEE matches against odds in 1857. He batted 25 times with 6 not outs and scored 97 runs at an average of 5.10. He bowled more than 840 overs, depending on which of various versions of bowling analyses you believe, and took no less than 204 wickets at a remarkably low cost. He cut a swathe through the local teams whose batsmen had rarely, if ever, faced a bowler of his pace, velocity and class.

The first match was at the Princes Park ground at Liverpool, beginning on 15 June, a match which the AEE won comfortably by 47 runs against a Liverpool Twenty-Two with Jackson bowling 20.3 overs and taking four for

13 in the second innings. On 18 June the team moved over to Manchester for a match against Twenty-Two of the Broughton Club whom they beat by an innings and 45 runs, with Jackson, now warming up and taking eight second innings wickets for 12 runs.

The next four matches brought Jackson seventy-six wickets, beginning with fourteen for 89 in 43.2 overs against Twenty-Two of Sleaford on 25 June, a game the AEE still managed to lose by nine wickets. The first five Sleaford batsmen made ducks with four of those who batted completing a pair in the second innings. Nine of the Sleaford men made ducks in this match out of the 36 who went in to bat. The men who did get some runs, most notably one of their given men, F.Tinley, with innings of 32 and 35, did enough to win the match.

If Jackson was disappointed with this result, his performance in the next match against Twenty-Two of Loughborough was truly outstanding. He bowled 57.3 overs to take eight for 52 as Loughborough scored 131, the AEE scoring 104 in reply. Jackson then took nine wickets for 11 runs in Loughborough's second innings of 78 for eighteen before rain caused the abandonment of the match. In his next match for the AEE on 6 July against Twenty-Two of Uppingham, Jackson did even better, taking 14 for 18 in the first innings and 11 for 19 in the second innings. This gave him match figures of twenty-five wickets for 37 runs in 56.1 overs. He bowled 20 batsmen, including six in seven balls in the Uppingham second innings. There was only one double figure score in Uppingham's two innings out of the 44 men who batted, 22 ducks being recorded in scores of 31 and 58. AEE only made 43 and 86 but still won by 43 runs.

There were another 22 ducks by the batsmen of Wakefield in Jackson's next game on 23 July, including two by Alfred Mynn, guesting for the local side, the first time that Mynn had recorded a pair since 1833, a remarkable sequence. A low- scoring match saw the AEE win by 13 runs, with Jackson recording figures of nine for 28 in 39.3 overs in the Wakefield first innings and eleven for 13 in the second in 38 overs, to clinch a win after the locals had been set no more than 47 to win.

On 30 July Twenty-Two of Derbyshire were beaten by five wickets, with Jackson taking nine for 31 in 30 overs in their first innings and one for 18 in the second. George Parr hit 67 in the AEE second innings, easily the most decisive batting contribution.

Moving into Lincolnshire in August the AEE faced Twenty-Two of Boston on 6 August, beating them by five wickets. Jackson shouldered another heavy stint of bowling, 86 overs in all, to take fourteen for 55 in the match. All four innings totals were in a range between 66 and 72. A comfortable win by eight wickets over Twenty-Two of Grantham on 20 August was notable for Heathfield Stephenson making 69 for AEE and Jackson bowling 73.1 overs and taking seventeen for 79, including thirteen for 37 in the second innings.

Jackson's workload was even heavier at Bradford in his next AEE match. He bowled no less than 64 overs in the Bradford first innings, taking ten for 40 as Bradford XXII made 129 all out. Isaac Hodgson and G.Atkinson bowled the AEE out for 66 and Jackson had to bowl a further 37 overs (101 in the match), taking four for 60 as Bradford ran up a score of 156 for ten before rain caused an abandonment. W.Wadsworth hit 55* for Bradford, W.Hirst made 36 and H.Lee 25. On 10 September a Leeds XXII containing a number of the same players who had just finished representing Bradford beat the AEE by 121 runs. Jackson had match figures of two for thirty-five. The AEE batting failed completely against the bowling of G.Atkinson - five for 9 in the first innings - and H.Lee with match figures of eleven for 38.

Jackson had a fine match against a Shropshire XXII at Aston Hall, Birmingham. He bowled 55 overs, taking twenty wickets for 30 and terrifying many of the local players on a bad pitch on which 20 ducks were recorded in the Shropshire innings and only one batsman reached double figures. Jackson also made the two highest scores in the match - 25 run out and 14*. The AEE won by eight wickets. At Stockton-on-Tees on 21 September Jackson sent down another 62.1 overs in the match, taking twelve wickets, but AEE lost to Stockton's XXII by seventeen wickets. Haygarth made a point about local team selection, stating that very few of the XXII had much connection with Stockton. G.Atkinson, I.Hodgson, R.Iddison and T.Hayward, who took nearly all the AEE wickets between them were all from the Bradford and Leeds area.

At North Shields on 24 September the AEE beat a local XXII by 30 runs, scores of 97 and 32 being good enough to outscore the local team's 49 and 50. Jackson took seventeen wickets in the match for 52 runs in 59.1 overs, bowling seven of the last eight batsmen in the second innings. Atkinson and Hodgson had another crack at the AEE, taking nine and six wickets respectively. The final game of the season took place at Richmond, North Yorkshire and was drawn very much in the AEE's favour. Jackson bowled 49 overs, taking ten for 42.

Earlier in the season Jackson, still coaching at Cambridge University, played for the Cambridge professionals against the Undergraduates who were perhaps being instructed too well, for they outplayed the professionals to such an extent that they actually gave up the match after the University had scored 149 and 200, and the professional side 125. Jackson took three wickets. At Bramall Lane on 22 June Jackson played for Nottingham against XVI of Sheffield, Nottingham winning by 9 runs. Jackson bowled 95.3 overs in the match and took nineteen for 105. R.C.Tinley hit 50 for Nottingham. Finally, Jackson played as a given man for the Household Brigade in a 12-a -side match against a team got up by the Earl of Stanford at the Earl's ground at Enville Hall. Stanford's side won by six wickets with Jackson taking eight wickets in the match as well as making his team's top score of 27 which was also Jackson's highest score of the season.

Altogether Jackson had taken 326 wickets in 1857 and was entitled to feel tired. He had also undergone a life-changing experience during the summer. He had got married.

Mahala Reavel (or Revel) was a Lincolnshire girl who was baptised at

CERTIFIED COPY OF AN ENTRY OF MARRIAGE — GIVEN AT THE GENERAL REGISTER OFFICE

Application Number 2004693-1

CERTIFIED to be a true copy of an entry in the certified copy of a register of Marriages in the Registration District of Spalding

Given at the GENERAL REGISTER OFFICE, under the Seal of the said Office the 1st day of February 2010

MXE 742719

CAUTION: THERE ARE OFFENCES RELATING TO FALSIFYING OR ALTERING A CERTIFICATE AND USING OR POSSESSING A FALSE CERTIFICATE. ©CROWN COPYRIGHT

WARNING: A CERTIFICATE IS NOT EVIDENCE OF IDENTITY.

A copy of John and Mahala Jackson's marriage certificate – 23 August 1857.

Swineshead, Lincolnshire on 29 December 1839. She was the daughter of Samual Revel, a publican, and his wife Ann. Mahala was eighteen years old when she married John Jackson, professional cricketer, at the parish church of Donington, Lincolnshire on 23 August 1857. Jackson had just finished a three day match at Grantham on 22 August and was due to play at Bramall Lane, Sheffield for the North against Surrey on 24 August, so the nuptials must have been short-lived, and any thoughts of a honeymoon must have been put on hold until the end of the cricket season as Jackson had few free dates.

The wedding certificate states that Mahala was eighteen, with John said to be 'of full age' which would mean 24 if we accept 1833 as his most likely birth year. Mahala was the daughter of a publican and it is possible that the couple met when the cricketer went for a drink at her father's hostelry at the end of a day's cricket to quench his considerable thirst. The young publican's daughter must have been impressed by the 6ft 1inch handsome gypsy, and his undoubted strength and obvious good looks would have helped cement their relationship.

It is hard to know just how much of their married life could have been spent together. John was playing cricket full time from April until as late as early October each year and he toured America and Canada in the winter of 1859/60 and Australia in 1863/4. In the 1870s he spent a summer in Ireland as professional to Lord Massereene's XI, and he had spells as a professional for two seasons at Burnley Cricket Club and fulfilled professional engagements at Cambridge and Richmond, North Yorkshire.

He can't have been at home a great deal and this may have helped keep the marriage going. When his cricket career finished, his marriage followed soon after.

The couple produced seven children. The eldest, Elizabeth, born in 1858, did not survive her teenage years but the others all grew up healthily. The eldest son, John, was born on 19 June 1861, followed by Kate (born 12 September 1863), Harry (born 29 March 1866), Samuel (born 1870), Lucie (born 16 January 1875 and Harold (born 1886).

From Census returns we can track Mahala living at 47, Wilson Street, Retford, Nottinghamshire in 1861, with her first born, Elizabeth, then aged two and John's mother, Margaret, whose age is given as 66, also resident there. John was not resident there at the time of the Census and may have been in Ireland at the time with the All-England Eleven, or perhaps at Cambridge coaching the students. The growing Jackson family stayed at Retford until 1870 when John found work as a caterer/groundsman/ professional cricketer at the Dingle Club in Liverpool. The family moved to Merseyside where their last two children, Lucie and Harold, were born. They appear on the 1871 Census living at 26, Smith Lane, Toxteth. Samuel, the latest addition to the family, was just six months old. John's mother, still lodging with them, is given as aged 82 which is clearly not correct as she was only 66 ten years earlier according to the 1861 return.

By the time of the 1881 Census the family were living at 23, Carlton Hill, Toxteth Park, Liverpool. Elizabeth had died by then and so had Margaret. The eldest son, John, now aged 19, was working as a labourer on the Liverpool docks, and Harry, 15, was a milk seller. Samuel, 11, and Lucie, 7, were still at school. John Jackson's cricketing career had by now run its course. He was close to 50 years of age and had never learnt to do anything other than play cricket. He was employed as a labourer in one of the warehouses on the Liverpool docks. This last, sad phase of his life will be dealt with in a later chapter. We must get back now to his cricket.

CERTIFIED COPY of an ENTRY OF BIRTH
Pursuant to the Births and Deaths Registration Act 1953

CK

Registration District East Retford

3. Birth in the Sub-district of Retford in the County of Nottingham

1 When and where born	2 Name, if any	3 Sex	4 Name and surname of father	5 Name, surname and maiden surname of mother	6 Occupation of father	7 Signature description and residence of informant	8 When registered	9 Signature of registrar	10* Name entered after registration
Twelfth September 1863 Alma Road East Retford	Kate	Girl	John Henry JACKSON	Mahala JACKSON formerly REAVILL	One of the Eleven of All England Cricketers	Mahala Jackson Alma Road East Retford	Twenty eighth September 1863	John Shadrack Piercy Registrar	/

Certified to be a true copy of an entry in a register in my custody

Hazel A Stephenson Superintendent Registrar

7/8/97

THIS CERTIFICATE IS NOT EVIDENCE OF THE IDENTITY OF THE PERSON PRESENTING IT.

Birth certificate of Kate Jackson. Jackson is described as 'One of the Eleven of All-England Cricketers. He was not trained to do anything else.

A group of John Jackson's descendants including his youngest daughter Lucie.

John Jackson at his son Samuel's wedding in 1891.

Chapter Five

Seasons of Plenty

Jackson played in 12 first-class matches in 1858, including two appearances for the Players against the Gentlemen. In the match at the Kennington Oval he took six for 55 and three for 53 in a Players victory by three wickets. In the match at Lord's the Players won with some ease by 285 runs. P.F.Warner described Jackson's bowling on a rough pitch as being 'demoralising'. He took five for 19 as the Gentlemen were dismissed for 52 in reply to the Players' first innings of 115. He took a further two wickets for 27 when the Gentlemen batted again, giving him sixteen wickets for 154 in the two matches. Lord's at this stage did not produce very good pitches.

There were two matches this season between the great professional Elevens, both played at Lord's. The first game beginning on 7 June was won by the UAEE by four wickets. Jackson scored 10 in the first AEE innings of 111 and then quickly removed Jem Grundy for 0 and John Lillywhite for 1 in UAEE's reply. Robert Carpenter was next man in and he treated the bowling, especially Jackson's, with a certain amount of disdain, driving and cutting the fast bowler for several boundaries. Jackson was less than impressed. He softened Carpenter up by hitting him on the back with a hard throw-in and then clean bowled the shaken batsman immediately afterwards for 45. William Caffyn scored 26 and UAEE led by 44 on first innings. Parr scored 52 for the AEE in their second innings of 143, but the UAEE got the 100 runs they needed to win for the loss of six wickets, with T.Hearne hitting 54*. Jackson bowled 60 overs in the match, finishing with five for 50 and two for 45. In the second match which commenced on 26 July and was played for the benefit of George Parr, Jackson's six for 40 and six for 28 helped the AEE to victory by an innings and 97 runs. Jackson also top-scored for the AEE with 45 in their only innings. The Duke of Malakaff, the French Ambassador, was present at the match and donated £1 to Parr's fund.

Jackson played one County match, for Nottinghamshire against Surrey at the Kennington Oval, taking five for 97 and one for 51, relatively expensive figures for him at this period of his career. Surrey won by nine wickets. It should be noted that Haygarth stated that the two Counties' scorebooks disagreed on the bowling figures, although Jackson's figures are not specifically mentioned as being in dispute.

The annual North v South fixture at Lord's saw the first appearance there of that fine Nottinghamshire batsman, Richard Daft. Jackson took eleven wickets in the match (six for 37 and five for 90), bowling 75 overs in all and hitting the stumps nine times. The South made 96 and 208, the North

215 and 90 for six, Jackson's scores being 9* and 33

At the Kennington Oval on 2 August the North began a three-day match against Surrey. The North led off with a score of 257. Surrey could only total 175 and had to follow on. They reached 253 all out, leaving the North to get 172 to win. They could only make 118, so Surrey won by 53 runs, a rare occasion of a side following on and winning a match. Jackson took five for 58 and two for 88 in a total of 78.1 overs.

In an era when most hits had to be 'run out', E.Stephenson stayed whilst 191 runs were scored and Parr ran every run between 7 and 164. Physical tiredness must have played a part in some dismissals. A.Diver for Surrey hit an all-run 7 and an all-run 6. Surrey had an unbeaten season, having already defeated an England side by an innings and 28 runs in a match notable for being the only occasion when a batsman, William Caffyn, hit a century in an innings in which Jackson bowled at him. Jackson did bowl him in the end for 102, finishing with figures of 37-13-79-3, having bowled twice as many deliveries as anyone else, although Haygarth stated there were other versions of the bowling figures. England scored 62 and 154, Surrey 244.

A first class match between the Single and the Married took place at the Kennington Oval on 9, 10 and 11 August with the Single men winning by 16 runs. Jackson played for the married men, of course, taking seven for 62 in 44.3 overs in the first innings, then four for 37 in 45.2 overs in the second thus giving him match figures of 11 for 99 in 44.3 overs in the first innings; then seven for 62 in 33 overs in the second. Haygarth commented on his very fast and straight bowling, with seven of the opposition being bowled.

On 20 September a match between Nottinghamshire and a combined Durham and Yorkshire team commenced at Stockton-on-Tees, the first County match to be played north of York. It was arranged under the auspices of Mr W.Richardson, a liberal supporter of the game in Stockton. The match was drawn, with the ground being saturated and unfit for further play after 3.00 pm on the third day. At the time Nottinghamshire needed only 25 more runs to win, with seven wickets in hand. Jackson once again bowled an enormous number of overs - 34 in the first innings and 43 in the second, taking five for 54 and two for 38. The combined counties' scores were 118 and 96, with Nottinghamshire making 140 (Jackson 15) and 51 for three.

Jackson appeared twice as a given man for Kent against an England XI. A two-day match at Lord's ended on the first day in an England victory by ten wickets as Kent collapsed despite the presence of such luminaries as Parr and Caffyn, as well as Jackson, for 33 and 41. Jackson took nine for 27 in England's first innings of 73. When the two teams met again at Canterbury on 16, 17 August, he took nine for 35 and made 26* to help Kent lead on first innings by 19 runs (104 to 85). Kent were dismissed for 103 in their second innings and Jackson's four for 55 in 25.2 overs could not stop England winning by five wickets.

Altogether Jackson bowled 702.2 overs in first-class matches with 260 maidens, and he took one hundred wickets for 1,116 runs He took five or more wickets in an innings 12 times, and ten or more in a match on three occasions.

Jackson appeared in 18 of the AEE matches against odds in 1858, of which seven were won, six lost and five left unfinished. A flavour of the itinerary can be got from the following list of his games. He played at Eastwell in Leicestershire on 10 June, Whitehaven in Cumbria on 14 June, Salford on 17 June and Chesterfield on 21 June. This amounted to a lot of travelling and he did a lot of bowling too: 232.1 overs in these matches, with 75 in an innings at Eastwell and 50 in an innings against Derbyshire. After some first-class matches, Jackson travelled on to Hull where he bowled another 83.2 overs in a match commencing on 28 June, and thence to Leeds on 8 July (73 overs there), Sleaford on 15 July (54 overs) and Newark on 29 July (71 overs).

After some more first-class cricket Jackson next appeared for the AEE at Luton on 12 August where he bowled 56 overs, Liverpool on 19 August (43 overs), Bradford on 23 August (41 overs), Grantham on 26 August (61 overs); then down to Truro to play Cornwall on 31 August (66.2 overs). Still the bowling and travelling were not finished. On 2 September the AEE should have played at Plymouth against East Cornwall and South Devon but, perhaps to Jackson's relief, rain ruined the match. On they went to Sheffield where Jackson bowled 99 overs against Hallam and Staveley on 6 September. Jackson's next match was at Rochdale where he played as a given man against the AEE on 9 September, bowling 55 overs. He returned to the AEE at Newport, Monmouthshire on 13 September, and from there to their final match of the season in front of Sir William Worsley's mansion at Hovingham, Yorkshire where Jackson bowled another 73.2 overs. The itinerary, and the fact that he was one of the main strike bowlers, offered little time for rest and recuperation other than anything bad weather might provide.

There is no doubt at all that John Jackson was chronically overbowled and that this hastened his retirement from the first-class game. In 1858 he had bowled 1,178.3 overs and taken 214 wickets. Often the devastation he caused was on an epic scale. At Newport, against Monmouthshire, he took twenty-four wickets for 61 runs, and at Hovingham he took twenty for 27, including an incredible nine wickets for 6 runs in 31.2 overs in the local team's second innings. At Truro, against Cornwall, he took sixteen for 30 and eight for 20; at Sleaford his figures were seven for 24 and eleven for 19. At Sheffield's Hallam and Staveley he took twelve for 25 and six for 38; yet this match is chiefly remembered for the feat of another bowler, H.H.Stephenson. Stephenson took three wickets with consecutive balls after which a collection was taken and the money used to buy the player a new hat. The term 'hat-trick' derived from this feat.

In other AEE matches Jackson took nine for 24 and seven for 38 against XVI of Oxford University, sixteen for 61 in the match against Newark, nine for 56 in 60 overs against Hull, nine for 43 in 50 overs against Derbyshire and nine for 63 in 56 overs against E.W. Vyse's team. It makes me weary just writing these figures down!

There were some unusual features in other AEE matches. At Eastwell, for example, the match was abandoned as a draw when a violent storm of wind and rain blew some of the tents over. Playing for the Manchester Broughton Club, one of the Club's given men, W.Swain, bowled 27 overs and conceded only 6 runs in the first innings of the AEE. The match at Hull was drawn with the Hull XXII only 4 runs short of victory, the scores being AEE 94 and 195; Hull 209 and 77 for five. In the drawn match at Leeds, Haygarth commented on the very fine analysis of John Jackson whose figures were 42 overs in the first innings and 31 in the second, taking, in all, twelve wickets for 45 runs At Grantham the local paper considered the match to be of sufficient importance as to merit an advertisement on the front page. In its report of the game the paper mentions shoddy fielding by the local men which gave away runs by aiming at the stumps rather than the wicketkeeper's gloves.

The *Liverpool Daily Post* report of the match at Liverpool describes Jackson as 'the finest and best fast bowler England can boast of'. At Truro Jackson took six wickets in 16 balls against batsmen unused to such terrifying bowling. *The West Briton* writes of batsmen wincing in pain after being hit by a Jackson delivery. At Newport a charge of 1/- admission was made and a grandstand and numerous tents were erected for spectators. At the conclusion of the match a dinner was held in honour of the AEE at the Westgate Hotel.

Jackson appeared in three other games as well. One was played for an England XI against Oxford University in a match which Jackson used to add fourteen wickets for 41 to his growing collection of scalps. He bowled 76.2.overs in this game. He played for a team of Old Cambridge Men against Cambridge University, taking seven wickets in this match, and he also appeared for an England XI against XVIII Veterans and took nine for 31. In a fantastic feat of endurance he had bowled more than 2040 overs in 1858 and taken 355 wickets. He was not a slow bowler and the sheer effort involved in bowling so many overs must have been tremendous.

John Jackson took part in ten first-class matches during the 1859 season, a season that was to culminate in the first ever English tour abroad. The two matches between Gentlemen and Players both finished in easy victories for the professionals who won by an innings and 25 runs at the Kennington Oval, and by 169 runs at Lord's. Jackson took five for 45 and four for 31 in the Oval match, and four for 41 and four for 28 in two impressive displays of fast bowling at Lord's, where he also made a hard-hitting 41 in the Players' first innings.

In the two matches between the great professional elevens, the AEE and the UAEE, he took fourteen for 61 in the match at Lord's on 6 and 7 June, a match which raised £100 for the benefit of the Cricketers' Fund. Eight of his first innings' victims were bowled. The United Eleven won, making 82 and 70 against AEE scores of 63 and 52. You might think this indicated a poor pitch and you would be quite right; Haygarth also commented on the heaviness of the ground after recent heavy rain, making it difficult to score quickly. The AEE batted for three and a half hours in their second innings. In the second match which began on 4 July Jackson met his old sparring partner, Carpenter, who hit 97 for UAEE and shared an opening stand of 149 with T.Hearne (62). Carpenter batted for four and a half hours as United made 262 in reply to the AEE's 165. The AEE could not make up the lost ground and scored only 130 in their second innings, leaving United to get the 34 they needed to win, for the loss of just one wicket. Jackson bowled 52 overs in the first innings of this match, taking three for 84, indifferent figures for him.

Jackson made just one appearance for Nottinghamshire in 1859, against Surrey, who were beaten at the Kennington Oval by eight wickets in a match in which George Parr made a fine 130. Jackson took six wickets in this match for 136 runs in 71.1 overs. Surrey's scores were 213 and 172, Nottinghamshire making 329 and 58 for two.

The North v South matches were among the highlights of the first-class season in the 1850s. In the match at Lord's on 27 and 28 June, the South won by ten wickets, with Haygarth scoring 45. *Bell's Life,* describing his innings, said that 'his defence against the terrific bowling of Jackson was beyond anything we ever saw'. Jackson bowled 67.2 overs to take four for 75 as the South scored 215. The North were bowled out for 107 and 115, and the South only needed eight to win. At Canterbury on 15 August, Jackson got some measure of revenge, although Haygarth did not play in this match. The North scores were 107 and 167, and the South were dismissed for 48 and 136, with Jackson and Jem Grundy being the only bowlers the North needed to use. Jackson took seven for 21 in 16.1 overs in the first innings and five for 53 in 42 overs in the second.

The North of England played Surrey twice, losing an interesting game at the Kennington Oval by two wickets, and the return at the Broughton Club ground in Manchester by 34 runs. In the match in Manchester the North batted with only ten men as their wicketkeeper, E.Stephenson, damaged his hand whilst trying to stop a thunderbolt from Jackson in Surrey's first innings. In the Oval match the North scored 234 and 123, with Surrey replying with 189 and 169 for eight. Jackson bowled 102.3 overs in the match, taking six for 72 and four for 68. At Manchester he shouldered a slightly lighter load, 91.3 overs, taking six for 71 and five for 54. Surrey made 189 and 112; the North scored 117 and 150.

A remarkable performance by V.E.Walker was the highlight of a victory for an England XI against Surrey at the Kennington Oval. Walker had a truly magnificent match, taking all ten Surrey wickets in their first inning, and then hitting a century (108), in England's second innings of 390. England, who had made 172 in their first innings, bowled Surrey out in one hour and 22 minutes for 39, with Jackson taking six for 21 and Walker four for 17. The result was a comprehensive win for England by 392 runs.

In all first-class matches in 1859 Jackson bowled 696 overs, 281 maidens and took 83 wickets for 919 runs at an average of 11.07. He took five or more wickets in an innings nine times, and on four occasions took ten or more wickets in a match.

Jackson played in 18 matches for the AEE in 1859, putting in another marathon stint, both in bowling and travelling, in which he bowled more than 1100 overs and took 262 wickets. The merry-go-round began at the Hyde Park ground in Sheffield on 30 May where the AEE lost to XXII of Hallam and Staveley by eighteen wickets. Jackson bowled 62 overs in the first Sheffield innings, taking eleven for 70. An unusual incident involving Jackson occurred when one of the local batsmen, G.Thorpe, had his wicket broken by Jackson in completing a run. He was given 'in' on appeal by the umpire but left his wicket, having assumed he was out. Jackson promptly pulled up a stump and Thorpe was then clearly out. The local paper mentions a protest by the AEE about the ground being watered overnight to the benefit of the local team. Sheffield denied this strenuously, but you would expect them to. The paper does not say how the matter was resolved.

In the next match against Manchester Broughton on 2, 3 and 4 June we find Haygarth once again bemoaning differences in the scorebooks, especially in the bowling analyses. Haygarth has Jackson bowling 36 overs and taking six for 53. The next game was at Fenny Stratford on 9,10 and 11 June, against XXII of Buckinghamshire, Jackson took three for 46 and eight for 24 in a total of 79 overs in an AEE victory. The first nine Buckinghamshire wickets fell for 7 runs in their second innings.

On 13, 14 and 15 June the AEE played XXII of Wiltshire at Salisbury, where Jackson bowled 37 overs in each innings and had figures of five for 39 and seven for 29. This was immediately followed by a match against XXII of Monmouthshire at Newport. Jackson's bowling was described by the local paper as 'deadly', as indeed it was. He took nine for 37 and eleven for 68 in a total of 76 overs, although the AEE still contrived to lose the match by 61 runs.

On 20 June the AEE caravan next appeared at Redruth in Cornwall, a match in which, you may recall, Jackson had terrified the local batsmen the year before. He repeated the medicine, taking ten wickets for 1 run in XXII of Cornwall's first innings of 22 which lasted only 45 minutes. He did not bowl in the second innings when Cornwall improved slightly, making 30, but the locals were clearly outmatched in a game in which George Parr hit a century. In a tribute to Jackson the *West Briton* declared: 'Cornwall witnessed the extraordinary and beautiful bowling of that Prince of Bowlers - John Jackson'. The AEE moved on to Wennington Park near Launceston to play XXII of East Cornwall and Devonshire on 23 June who were also rolled over by Jackson. His figures of ten for 10 in 27 overs ensured another comfortable win for the AEE. The XXII made 58 and 33 all out, and the difference in class between them and the AEE was clearly apparent.

Jackson's next match for the AEE was on 7 and 8 July at Ipswich in Suffolk where he had been the club professional in the early 1850s. He showed his liking for the wicket by taking fourteen for 18, and seven for 22, bowling a total of 71.3 overs. He dismissed one of the Ipswich openers with a 'Terrifier' (local paper). At Sleaford the local XXII were disposed of by Jackson and Heathfield Stephenson with more 'Terrific' bowling, Jackson's 56 overs in the match bringing him twenty wickets for 40 runs. Fifteen of Jackson's victims were bowled which gives some indication of his consistent accuracy. At Derby he starred with the bat, scoring 31 in the first AEE innings of a drawn match in which he also took eight wickets, although the bowling analysis is incomplete.

The next AEE game in which Jackson appeared was at Oakham in Rutland on 7 and 8 July, where 4,000 attended each day, with excellent entertainment being provided by a brass band. Jackson destroyed the local side's batting once again, taking twelve for 21 in 39 overs in their first innings, and seven for 32 in 41.1 overs in their second. Jackson then appeared at Sleaford where he had match figures of 20 for 40 in 56 overs. This was followed by an eight wicket haul against XXII of Derbyshire. There were 18 more wickets in a match at Oakham against XXII of Rutland. This form continued into August at the Edge Hill ground in Liverpool where Jackson took sixteen wickets for 71 in 70 overs in another hostile display, and in the next match, at Cambridge where he bagged ten for 40 and ten for 28 in 94.1 overs, besides taking five catches. This was followed by figures of seven for 24 and ten for 22 against XXII of Grantham.

Moving on to Devizes Jackson proceeded to decimate XXII of North Wiltshire, taking eleven for 20 and six for 27 in a total of 55.3 overs. Then on 22, 23 and 24 August it was down to Hove to play XXII Gentlemen of Sussex where Jackson sealed an AEE victory with ten for 59 in the second innings of the Gentlemen. Rain at Bradford on 30 and 31 August offered the AEE some welcome time off. There was no play at all on the first day and only 30 minutes on the third. Jackson took six for 11 in 21 overs with Haygarth again complaining that there were other versions of the bowling figures about. In the AEE's final match of the season against XXII of Rochdale, the Lancashire locals suffered badly at Jackson's hands, the great fast bowler taking ten for 25 and nine for 25 in the course of bowling 75.1 overs. He must have heaved a sigh of relief that all the hard work was over.

If, however, Mahala hoped to see more of him now that cricket was finished for the season, she was sadly mistaken. The first English overseas tour was about to take place and her husband must have been one of the first names to be selected for it.

Chapter Six

With George Parr's Team in the USA and Canada 1859

At the conclusion of the 1859 cricket season twelve English professional cricketers were chosen to cross the Atlantic Ocean and undertake a short tour of Canada and America. The tour was arranged by the Montreal Cricket Club, the leading cricketing body in America and by the Cricketers Friendly Society in England. The Montreal Club guaranteed that each of the twelve players would receive £50 plus the whole of any expenses they might incur.

The twelve players selected comprised the pick of the AEE and UAEE teams, six players from each being chosen. From Nottinghamshire came George Parr, the captain, Jem Grundy, and, of course, John Jackson; from Sussex John Wisden and John Lillywhite; from Cambridgeshire Tom Hayward, Robert Carpenter and Alfred John Diver; and from Surrey Heathfield Stephenson, Julius Caesar, William Caffyn and Tom Lockyer.

The team set sail from Liverpool on 7 September on the *Nova Scotia* and suffered a rough crossing of 15 days in various stages of discomfort before casting anchor in the St Lawrence River on 21or 22 September. At one stage the waves were so high that John Wisden suggested that the seas 'could do with a touch of the heavy roller' but they finally disembarked safely and got down to business.

The team's series of matches began in Montreal on 24 September against XXII of Lower Canada whom they beat by eight wickets, with Jackson bowling 70.1 overs in the match to take thirteen for 42. He had announced himself in style to his hosts. This was followed by a supplementary match in which the six of the UAE and five locals took on the six of the AEE and five more locals. Jackson took three for 48 in a match curtailed by rain.

At Hoboken, New York, watched by a huge crowd of 2,500, the team beat XXII of USA by an innings and 64 runs on 3, 4 and 5 October, with Jackson's 28 overs bringing him eleven for 11 or ten for 10. There was another supplementary match between T.Lockyer's side and H.H.Stephenson's side, in the course of which Jackson hit Parr on the arm thus putting him out of action for the rest of the tour. After the match a dinner was held in the English team's honour at Astor House.

Three days later, in Philadelphia, Jackson took eight for 37 in 59 overs and seven for 7 in 16, as England beat XXII of Philadelphia by seven wickets. There was yet another supplementary match between Five of the South of England with six Americans and Five of the North of England which was

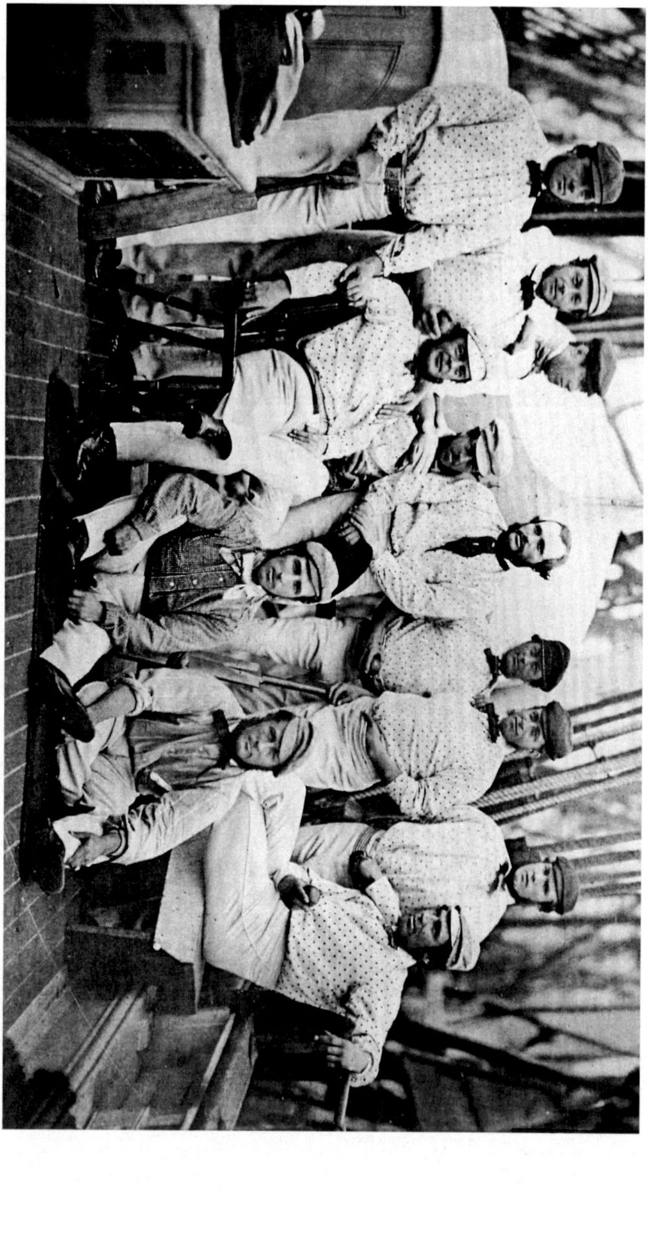

George Parr's team to North America 1859
Back row:(l to r) R.Carpenter, W.Caffyn, T.Lockyer, J.Wisden, G.Parr, J.Grundy, J.Caesar, T.Hayward, J.Jackson.
Front row: A.J.Diver, John Lillywhite. [Roger Mann Collection]

curtailed by rain. The England players were given a grand banquet in the Girard Guard House, Philadelphia and on the following day the team had time to visit the Niagara Falls.

At Hamilton the team beat a local XXII by ten wickets. Jackson had a relatively quiet game, bowling only 27 overs, which perhaps explains why he was allowed to open in England's second innings, with just 41 needed to win. He finished the match 16 not out. The side's last match saw them play a combined USA/Canada XXII at Rochester and beat them by an innings and 68 runs. Jackson took nine wickets for 38 in this match in 37.2 overs. The match was played in desperately cold weather with the fielders muffled up in gloves and greatcoats. Sounds like the average English April. Altogether in these tour matches Jackson took 52 wickets and bowled 237.3 overs, a typical workload for this big-hearted bowler.

On Saturday 29 October the team set sail for Liverpool on the mail screw steamer *North Briton* and endured another rough crossing before they finally berthed in Liverpool on 11 November. They had covered, in all, about 7,500 miles and made history. Haygarth recorded that 'each man cleared about £90, free of all expenses, *besides presents*'.

Chapter Seven
At the Height of His Powers

The season of 1860 was a particularly wet and dismal one. Haygarth's *Scores and Biographies* says bluntly that: 'the season was, as regards weather, one of the worst, perhaps, that cricketers have had to encounter'. Match after match was disrupted.

For John Jackson, still fulfilling his professional duties at Cambridge University, the season began on 3 and 4 May with the annual encounter between the Undergraduates and the Players engaged to coach them. The Undergraduates won by 81 runs with Jackson taking three wickets and scoring 0 and 10. On 18 and 19 May he played as a given man for XXII of Reigate against the UAEE in a match ruined by rain, which should have begun on 17 May had the ground not been waterlogged. The UAEE were bowled out for 108 with Jackson taking six for 39 in 57 overs, but Reigate were bowled out for 56 by Walker and Grundy. Jackson took two for 20 in the UAEE second innings of 60, but rain returned when Reigate were 51 for five, putting paid to any chance of a finish.

Jackson took part in 13 first-class matches in 1860, in which he bowled 751 overs, 308 of which were maidens, taking 109 wickets for 9.20. He took five or more wickets in an innings eleven times, and ten or more in a match on five occasions.

The Players won both of their encounters with the Gentlemen in 1860, winning at the Kennington Oval by eight wickets and, rather more comprehensively at Lord's, by an innings and 181 runs. The feature of the Oval match which began on 5 July was a brilliant innings of 119 by Robert Carpenter who hit one delivery clean out of the ground, a feat never performed before at the ground when the wickets were pitched in the centre of the playing area. He also had another big hit which landed near the top of the pavilion. Jackson's batting efforts were more modest, 13* and 11, but he bowled 38.2 overs in the Gentlemen's first innings, taking four for 46. In their second knock he did not take a wicket in 37 overs from which 73 runs were scored. It was a rare occasion for Jackson to remain wicketless after bowling so many overs. Haygarth does mention that the bowling analyses in other accounts differ from his. The Players made 328 and 80 for two, the Gentlemen scoring 160 and 245.

In the Lord's match which began on 9 July, Tom Hayward hit 132 for the Players, with E.Willsher coming in ninth and making 73, and John Lillywhite, eighth, hitting 66. The total reached 394. John Jackson then bowled out three of the Gentlemen's top six batsmen who made 6 runs between them in taking three for 54 in 35 overs as the amateurs were all out for 137. In their follow-on only two bowlers were needed - Jackson and Willsher - as the Gentlemen crumbled to 76 all out. Jackson took four for 32 in 25 overs. It was a fairly one-sided encounter.

The first game between the great professional elevens took place at Lord's on 28, 29 and 30 May for the benefit of the Cricketers Fund and raised £150 for that worthy cause. The AEE were victors by 21 runs. Jackson made 12* and 29, the 29 being his best score of the season. He took four for 42 and four for 41 in a match total of 79 overs. It was George Parr's turn to hit a ball out of one of the major grounds, putting a huge square-leg hit over the Tavern off the bowling of William Caffyn. Parr's second innings of 55 was easily the highest score of the match in which the AEE totals were 71 and 131, while UAEE made 89 and 92.

The second match between the Elevens began on 19 July and was drawn. It was the first game between the Elevens to be played at the Kennington Oval. The AEE scored 156 (Jackson 2), and 221 (Jackson 4). The UAEE replied with 123, Jackson taking three for 58 off 35 overs. The UAEE needed 255 to win, and Jackson made a monumental effort to win the match for his side. He sent down 40 overs and took seven of the eight wickets that fell, conceding 40 runs. When stumps were drawn, the UAEE were 102 for eight.

In county matches Nottinghamshire played home and away fixtures against Surrey. In the match at the Kennington Oval Jackson had the outstanding figures of six for 34 and nine for 49 in the Surrey innings and was rewarded with a collection, the proceeds being presented to him by the Surrey Club secretary. None of the Surrey players looked comfortable against him and he dismissed the first nine in the order in the second innings. He clearly won the match for Nottinghamshire whose scores of 83 and 105 were enough to beat the Surrey totals of 66 and 107 by 15 runs. It was rare indeed for a bowler to take fifteen wickets in an eleven-a-side match.

At Trent Bridge in the return match on 26 July, Surrey had some revenge, winning by 30 runs with their star batsman, William Caffyn, hitting 91 in the second innings, despite a fierce assault by Jackson who knocked the bat out of Caffyn's hand and struck him a severe blow on the knee with the next ball. Jackson finished with one for 22 and five for 78 off 53 overs, as Surrey made 109 and 247. The Nottinghamshire scores were 196 and 130.

A 'Champion's' match was played on the Old Trafford ground on 7, 8 and 9 June between the England XI which was made up of players who had toured America and Canada, and 'Another' England XI made up from players who had not. On a heavy and wet ground the lobs of R.C.Tinley were decisive. He took fourteen wickets for 59 runs for the 'other' England XI. Jackson took five for 19 and five for 38 in reply for the England XI, but the 'other' team won by three wickets. England made 83 and 57; 'Another' England scored 40 and 101 for seven.

A match played at Lord's on 24 and 25 July featured an Eleven of England (first chosen) pitted against a Next XIV in a match that the XIV won by eight wickets. The Eleven made 130 and 57 with R.C.Tinley taking seven for 35, a vital and match-winning contribution, given the low-scoring nature of the game. Jackson bowled heroically for 40.1 overs to take eight for 62 and give England a lead on first innings as the XIV were dismissed for 128, but Tinley's response left the XIV needing only 60 to win, and they made these for the loss of five wickets, despite Jackson taking another three for 30 in 25 overs.

In a match at the Kennington Oval on 30 and 31 July the North beat Surrey by an innings and 14 runs with Jackson and Tinley the only bowlers the North needed to use in the Surrey innings of 51 and 106. Jackson took seven for 57 in 56.2 overs, but he was outshone by Tinley who took twelve for 93. The North scored 171. Bad weather severely interfered with the return match between the two sides at the Broughton ground in Salford with only one hour's play being possible on the second day. Jackson took eight for 54 in 37 overs in Surrey's first innings of 113, and five for 46 as they made 123 for eight at the second attempt. The North scored 108 in their only innings.

Rain also disrupted the match at the Kennington Oval between England and Surrey on 6, 7 and 8 August. The third day was washed out completely and the game abandoned as a draw.Jackson scored 17 and took one wicket.

At Canterbury on 13 and 14 August XVI of Kent beat England by an innings and 48 runs. Jackson took nine for 34 in Kent's 152, but E.Willsher of Kent did even better, taking eight for 16 in 41 overs and three for 14 in 20 overs, while England could only score 64 and 40. Haygarth described Willsher's bowling as 'something wonderful'. Jackson's other first-class engagement this season ended in a victory for the North over the South by 53 runs. The match was played on 17 and 18 September at Sleaford in Lincolnshire, a neutral venue if ever there was one. The North scored 127 and 63, and the South were dismissed for 90 and 47. Jackson bowled 48 overs in the match, taking eight wickets for 57. Haygarth noted that the South were missing such players as Caffyn who had an injured leg, and Lockyer who was ill.

John Jackson took part in 14 of the AEE matches against odds in 1860. He batted 22 times with two not outs and scored 161 runs at an average of 8.05. He bowled 507.3 overs, less than half the number he bowled in 1859, which is somewhat indicative of the wet summer which rendered his pace less effective. He still took 110 wickets at a cost of 445 runs, however, not a bad return at all, and he took ten wickets or more in an innings five times, and fifteen wickets in a match once.

His most devastating performance came on 18, 19 and 20 June at the New Ground, Nettleham Road, Lincoln in the shadow of the magnificent cathedral. He took ten wickets for 20 in 40 overs in the first innings of XXII of Lincolnshire, and twelve for 19 in the second innings in 32 overs, as the locals were bowled out for 60 and 34, with only three double figures recorded out of 44 innings by the Lincolnshire batsmen. Sadly it did not result in a win for the AEE as the two professional bowlers, R.C.Tinley and W.Slinn who were guesting for the Lincolnshire side, bowled the AEE out for 37 and 46, only George Anderson mastering the conditions with a score of 25 in the second innings. Lincolnshire won by 11 runs. New ground, new pitch, (not bedded in?). The score seemed very low with only four innings out of 66 reaching double figures.

Jackson began his season with the AEE at Bath on 4 June with a match against the Lansdown Club who included E.M.Grace in their team. Jackson demolished the locals in a 30 over spell in which he took seven wickets for 10 runs. Lansdown, playing without any professional help, were out for 28 (top score 7; 10 men made ducks). Grace had made 21* in the Club's second innings of 67 for eight when the match was rained off. Jackson had by this stage taken three for 12 in 17 overs. The AEE scores, on a ground made heavy by recent rain, were 75 and 77.

Following the defeat at Lincoln, mentioned above, the Eleven moved on to Salford where they were defeated by XX of Manchester Broughton Club by eleven wickets on 21, 22 and 23 June. J.Makinson made 104 for the local side, one of very few hundreds ever recorded against the great professional sides. Jackson took some punishment but still finished with eleven for 75 in 67.3 overs as well as making the top score of 26* in the AEE's second innings of 99. Manchester Broughton owed much to Makinson whose century came in a total of 180 that contained only two other double figure scores. The AEE hit 117 in their second innings, setting the local side 37 to win. Jackson took three for 31 in 9.3 overs as the locals chased this total down.

Some dreadful weather at the Chuckery Ground, Walsall, led to the match against a Walsall XXII on 25, 26 and 27 June ending in a draw. Walsall only batted once, with Jackson taking the opportunity of snaffling twelve more wickets for 26 in 42 overs. The AEE game against XXII of Monmouthshire at Newport on 28, 29 and 30 June was played out on another heavy ground with play being much delayed and interrupted by rain and showers. The AEE won the match with Jackson taking twelve for 25 in the Monmouthshire second innings in 45.2 overs.

His other great performance was at Barnsley on 20 August when, in 42 overs, he took thirteen wickets for 27 in a match against a Barnsley XXII. This match occasioned great interest with a total of 8,000 spectators attending and gate receipts totalling £120. A gala took place after the match complete with a brass band accompaniment. Only one Barnsley player managed to reach double figures as the local side were bowled out for 46 and 44. Eleven ducks were recorded. The AEE made 134 in their innings and won by an innings and 44 runs.

The AEE were beaten by a Yorkshire XXII at York on 2, 3 and 4 July, before defeating XXII of Gainsborough by 49 runs on 12, 13 and 14 July. One of the local players, G.E.Cotterill, made one huge hit in the course of his first innings of 31 which measured 122 yards from the wicket to the pitch. Jackson took two wickets for 31 at Gainsborough, having taken six for 54 against Yorkshire. At Sheffield on 16, 17 and 18 July the AEE met XVIII

The All-England Eleven at Gainsborough 1860.
[Newark CC]

of the Sheffield Hallam Club, beating them by an innings and 156 runs after hitting up a score of 339 (a considerable total to make against odds), by consistent batting in front of a crowd of 4,000 which included many aristocratic patrons. Jackson's contribution was to take five for 33 in the first innings, but was overshadowed by R.C.Tinley who took ten for 20 and all seventeen for 58.

On 2, 3 and 4 August the AEE next played at a new venue, Shugborough Park, on the Earl of Lichfield's estate, where they comfortably beat a local XXII by nine wickets. Jackson took two for 10 and three for 4 in 25.2 overs. Another new venue was Dunstable on 9 and 10 August where the AEE won by ten wickets against XXII of Bedfordshire, with Tinley taking eighteen wickets and Jackson three for 29. This was another heavy ground, more suited to Tinley's guile than to Jackson's pace.

At Macclesfield in Cheshire, the team ran into more bad weather in a drawn match on 16 and 17 August. E.J.Bousfield scored 50 for Macclesfield XXII with Jackson taking five for 31 in 24 overs. Injury prevented him from bowling at Plymouth where the AEE beat XXII of Cornwell and Devon by nine wickets on 27, 28 and 29 August. Jackson had either sprained his ankle or his side which meant that he was unable to play in the next match.

The AEE next played a match in Glasgow against XXII of the Caledonian Club which they lost by 20 runs. It was late in the season now, 20, 21 and 22 September Jackson took one for 9 in 12 overs, but Tinley had another crop of victims, taking twenty-six wickets with his lobs for 78 runs.

Jackson's only other appearance in the 1860 season was at Sheffield where he played for Nottingham in a rain-ruined match against XVI of Sheffield on 11 and 13 June. He took eight for 23 in Sheffield's first innings in 23.1 overs, and three for 27 in 40 overs in the second. Tinley was the only other bowler that Nottingham used.

In all matches Jackson had added a further 238 wickets to his growing tally which represented a remarkable achievement in such a wet season where the wickets rarely had any pace and were much more suited to slow bowlers.

Jackson played in fourteen first-class games in the 1861 season. Still at the height of his powers, he took 81 wickets at an average of 13.50. He bowled 598.2 overs, conceding 1094 runs. On nine occasions he took five or more wickets in an innings, and twice he took ten or more wickets in a match.

One of his finest performances was in the Players match against the Gentlemen at Lord's on 1 and 2 July in which he took six for 31 in 17 overs in the first innings of the amateurs, and five for 68 in the second in 31.3 overs. He bowled unchanged throughout both innings with E.Willsher, and it should be pointed out that as the Gentlemen followed on, this meant that he bowled 48.3 overs consecutively from one end. It was very rare for only two bowlers to be used by a side in an eleven-a-side match. The Players scored 246 and the Gentlemen replied with 70 and 116, the Players winning by an innings and 60 runs. The professionals duly completed the 'double' over the amateurs at The Oval on 4, 5 and 6 July, winning that match by an innings and 68. The Players amassed 358. The Gentlemen failed with the bat, making 154 and 136. Jackson did little bowling, only 5 overs for 10 runs in the first innings, and 6 overs to take one for 14 in the second.

The first of the great tussles between the professional Elevens took place at Lord's on 3, 4 and 5 June again for the benefit of the Cricketers Fund Friendly Society, raising a sum of £137.9s. A very close and exciting match was won by the AEE by a mere 5 runs. The AEE were bowled out for 74 with Caffyn taking five for 41 and W.Buttress four for 29, but Jackson blasted out the UAEE, bowling 24.2 overs and taking seven for 31 in an innings of 61 all out in a great display of hostile fast bowling. Three of the UAEE players scored 8; nobody reached double figures. Unexpectedly leading by 13, the AEE fared better in their second innings with Richard Daft scoring 48, George Anderson 24 and John Jackson a hard-hit 41. The total was 152 and the UAEE needed 106 to win. G.Griffith made 45, R.Carpenter 29, and the total was 160 for nine, or 6 needed to win when the last of the UAEE batsmen was run out. Jackson had taken two for 55 in 27 overs.

The return match was played at Old Trafford, Manchester 11, 12 and 13 July and was badly interrupted by rain which allowed only ten minutes play on the first day. The match was played for the benefit of the two Elevens with each player receiving over £10 per man. Jackson taking five for 64 off 25 overs. In a third match at The Oval on 5, 6 and 7 August, the UAEE won by 115 runs. Jackson bowled 13 overs in the UAEE second innings, taking two for 40.

Jackson took part in two county matches for Nottinghamshire in 1861, both against Surrey and both lost. At The Oval on 6, 7 and 8 July Surrey won by 103 runs, scoring 168 and 203, with Jackson bowling 62.2 overs and taking five for 77 and three for 54. Nottinghamshire scored 130 and 138. Surrey duly completed the 'double' at Trent Bridge on 25, 26 and 27 July where Jackson took three for 36 and nought for 23 in 32 overs. Nottinghamshire suffered a batting failure, making 134 and 79, with Surrey scoring 136 and 78 for two to win by eight wickets.

Jackson played in four matches for the North of England in 1861. Against the South of England at Lord's on 15, 16 and 17 July, he took two for 49 in 41.2 overs, and four for 47 in 31 as the South scored 195 and 94 for six to win the match by four wickets. Caffyn, who played a number of fine innings against 'Jackson' sides this year, scored 65 in the South's first innings. The North could only muster 14 and 139 in their innings'. At Aston Park, Birmingham, on 5, 6 and 7 September, the sides met again on a ground Haygarth condemned as 'terribly rough, quite unfit for cricket'. He clearly was not impressed! Jackson took advantage of the conditions to take six for 43 and five for 40 in a total of 58.1 overs, but it was not enough to win the game. The South made 86 and 122, beating the North totals of 100 and 65 by 43 runs.

At the Kennington Oval on 18, 19 and 20 July, the North took on Surrey in an interesting match that was won by Surrey by 92 runs. Surrey scored 142 (Jackson one for 35) and the North replied with 250, Daft hitting 64, Hayward 66 and Carpenter 62. Behind by 108 runs, Surrey owed much to Caffyn who scored 98 whilst Lockyer hit 69* and G.Griffith 59. Their total was 320 with Jackson bowling 58 overs to take three for 97. The North needed 213 to win but collapsed to 120 all out, with Jackson making the highest score of 30.

In the return match at Manchester Broughton's ground, the weather washed out the first day, 22 August. On the designated second day the North scored 163 and Surrey replied with 184 (G.Griffith 59, Jackson seven for 51 off 36 overs). Fresh wickets were then prepared as those used in the two sides' first innings had been badly cut up and affected by the rain that had fallen. When play resumed the North went in again and scored 162 for five with E.Stephenson hitting 69.

Caffyn was the star batsman again when an England side met Surrey at The Oval on 29 August. He scored 58 and 46 despite being somewhat lame. Surrey scored 234 and 229 with E.Dowson making their highest score of 80. Jackson took three for 78 and one for 67, one of his leaner returns. England made 189 and 218 to bring the total number of runs scored in the match to 870, but Surrey won by 56 runs.

At the Lord's ground on 8 July a match was played between an England XI and Fifteen of Kent which the Kent side won by the margin of an innings and 74 runs. Jackson bowled 27 overs to take four for 45 in the Kent innings of 243 with England making 84 and 85 in their two innings. In the return match at Canterbury Kent played with 14 men and won by 54 runs. Jackson bowled only 4 overs for 21 runs in Kent's 134 all out but, after

The All-England Eleven 1861. Standing (l to r): E.Willsher, H.H.Stephenson, G.Parr, ?, T.Hayward, G.F.Tarrant, G.Anderson, R.C.Tinley, J.Jackson. On ground: A.Clarke, R.P.Carpenter [Roger Mann Collection]

England had been dismissed for 98, Jackson had a burst of 19 overs to take six for 18 as Kent made 148 in their second innings. England, needing 185 to win, could only total 130.

John Jackson took part in 19 of the All-England Eleven matches in 1861. He batted 30 times, being not out in four innings, and he scored 209 runs at an average of 8.03. He bowled more than 550 recorded overs (in some cases the exact analyses have been lost in the mists of time), and he took 121 wickets, fifteen wickets in a match three times. There were some prodigious bowling feats, his best return being eighteen wickets for 65 runs in an early season match against XXII Irishmen on 20, 21 and 22 May. He bowled 77.3 overs in this match. In the previous game, when the AEE played at the Coburg Gardens, Dublin on 16, 17 and 18 May, a match graced by the presence of the Lord Lieutenant of Ireland, Jackson had taken seventeen wickets, bowling thirteen of them. This match was against XXII Officers of Ireland, one of whom, a Captain Hunter, was listed as 'absent' in the second innings. No reason of absence is given. Both these games were won by the AEE by eight wickets.

Returning to England, the AEE were scheduled to begin their first match at Bath against the Lansdown Club on 23 May, the day after their final game in Dublin had finished. There was, you can see, no rest period for the, no doubt, weary cricketers. Understandably the AEE were dismissed for 75 in their first innings and went on to lose to the local XXII by thirteen wickets. Jackson took seven wickets in the match. Although the exact analysis is not given, but he is known to have bowled E.M.Grace for 0 in his second innings.

The AEE went on to lose their next match too, against XXII of Bradford, another long journey from Bath although there was a day's break between these two matches unlike those in Dublin and Bath. They lost by 17 runs with Jackson taking two for 8 in 15 overs and six for 36 in 42 overs, while the local paper praised the fielding of the AEE men, particularly that of Jackson, Tinley, Tarrant and Carpenter, which frequently gained much merited applause from an appreciative crowd.

On 10 June the AEE played a match for R.C.Tinley's benefit at Burton-on-Trent where they beat a local XXII by an innings and 75 runs. Jackson took twelve wickets in the Burton-on-Trent first innings but did not bowl in their second knock.

The next game was at Shugborough Park on 13, 14 and 15 June where the side lost by five wickets to a XXII got up by the Earl of Lichfield. Jackson bowled 63 overs in the match, taking three for 17 and six for 21. An interesting tale relating to this match was told by Richard Daft in his book, *Kings of Cricket.* He stated that on one of the days allotted to the match, Lord Lichfield gave his visitors permission to fish a piece of water in the park, called 'The Stew'. Parr is said to have caught a number of pike in a short space of time. He sent one of the largest to a friend in Nottingham and, on the pike being opened, a whole rat was found in its stomach.

Remaining in the Midlands the AEE played and beat a XXII of Walsall by an innings and 177 runs on 17, 18 and 19 June. Richard Daft hit 114 and Tom Hayward 60 as the AEE rattled up 305. Jackson was not required to bowl as Tinsley and Hayward bowled Walsall out for 50 and 78. Large crowds attended each day with special trains bringing regular and numerous passengers from the surrounding districts to watch the game. The Rifle Corps Band was there to keep the crowd entertained during intervals of play, but there were complaints about the dirt in the lane leading up to the Chuckery ground which, it was felt, the town authorities might have done more to dampen down.

As soon as the match finished, the AEE rushed to catch a train to Nottingham whence they were due to go on to Grantham for their next match starting the following day against Captain H.E.Handley's XVIII, a game which the AEE won by 34 runs. Jackson had the amazing figures of four for 6 in 11 overs as he proved himself the match- winner at the crux of the game.

The highlight of the AEE's next match against XVIII of Manchester Broughton Club which began on 27 June was the wonderful bowling of Edgar Willsher who bowled at one stage 25 consecutive overs for just one run. Jackson bowled well too, 54 overs in the match bringing him seven wickets for 78 runs. The Club beat the AEE by three wickets.

John Jackson spent most of the following month playing in the first-class matches. He returned to AEE duties on 22 July at Chesterfield where the AEE beat XXII of Derbyshire by seven wickets, with Jackson dismissing 26 batsmen for 44 runs in 74 overs. Only one player reached double figures and there were 16 noughts.

A trip up to Glasgow on 1 August saw Jackson take six for 25 in 42 overs against XXII of the Glasgow Caledonian Club in a drawn match. On 8 August the AEE played Captain Handley's XXII at Barton Court near Hungerford, losing by thirteen wickets. In the next match, at Lincoln on 15, 16 and 17 August, Jackson was slightly injured in a collision with the Lincolnshire batsman, E.A.Howson, and could not bowl in the county's second innings. He had taken three for 25 in their first innings in 21 overs. The AEE won by nine wickets.

On 29, 30 and 31 August at Gainsborough Richard Daft achieved the feat of carrying his bat through an AEE innings, batting for six and a half hours and scoring 67*. A collection for Daft raised £3.10s. In a match in which Jackson did not bowl attendances were 600 on the first day, 900 on the second day and 200 on the third day with a total of £3.12s.6d in gate receipts. The AEE captain, George Parr, objected to the presence of Rowbotham as a given man for Gainsborough, and the start of play was delayed whilst the matter was resolved. It was finally agreed that W.Prest should take Rowbotham's place in the side. The AEE won by an innings and 40 runs.

Two days later on 2 September after another long journey the AEE took the field on the Broadwater ground in Godalming, Surrey, where the AEE beat XXII of Godalming, Guildford and District by 22 runs. Jackson bowled 41 overs in the match, taking three wickets for 40 runs. Haygarth maked the somewhat tart comment that 'as Mudie, Lockyer, Baker and co were not shown as being given men, even though they clearly were, the district must have been rather large'. Six of the local team were run out.

Playing against XX of the Sheffield, Hallam and Staveley Club on the Hyde Park Ground in Sheffield on 9, 10 and 11 September, Jackson's contribution was mainly with the bat. He scored only 10 (run out) in the AEE second innings but he helped R.C.Tinley add 70 for the last wicket, vital runs as they only won the match by 54. Tinley's hard hitting in his innings of 80 was loudly cheered by the crowd of 2,000. Then it was straight off to Chatham in Kent where the AEE beat XVIII of Chatham and District by 96 runs with George Tarrant and R.C.Tinley proving too strong for the Chatham side.

The last of Jackson's AEE matches was at Middlesbrough on 16, 17 and 18 September where Jackson bowled 14 overs to take two for 11. In truth he had not bowled much since his collision with Howson in the game at Lincoln. Nevertheless the local Middlesbrough paper was full of praise, speaking of 'fast and furious bowling from as fine a handler of the ball as ever saw leather'. Jackson also struck 35 in quick time when AEE batted. The principal tradesmen of the town shut their shops to give their employees a chance of watching the game, enjoyment of which was marred by very cold weather and frequent showers.

Jackson played in two of the Nottinghamshire trial games, one as early as 1 April when the county side played XXII of Nottinghamshire Colts, beating the youngsters by an innings and 47 runs, with Jackson taking ten wickets. On 26, 27 and 28 August, the Nottinghamshire First Eleven played a match against the next XXII of Nottinghamshire for the benefit of George Butler, winning by five wickets, with Jackson taking fifteen for 78 in 77 overs in the match.

On 24, 25 and 26 June at Lord's, Eleven Players of England played a match against XVI Undergraduates of Oxford and Cambridge, winning by ten wickets. Jackson took four for 64 in 27 overs. He played one match as a given man, turning out for XXII of Bishop Auckland and helping them to an eight wicket win over Cambridgeshire, dismissing five batsmen in each innings for 36 and 33 respectively in a total of 52.1 overs.

On 20 October 1861 an English team set out on the inaugural tour of Australia. Each man was offered the sum of £150 plus expenses to go on tour, but a number of the best professionals including John Jackson could not agree terms with the promoters, Messrs Spiers and Pond. One of the main sticking points was the preponderance of Surrey players in the team which was to be captained by Surrey's Heathfield Stephenson. The Northern professionals expressed a preference for the captain of the All-England Eleven, George Parr, to be captain but, as the Surrey Secretary, C.W.Alcock, was making most of the arrangements, this was not likely to be agreed and, as a result, Jackson, Parr and several other players missed an historic opportunity.

John Jackson took part in 14 first-class matches in 1862. He batted 20 times, being not out in six innings, and he scored 362 runs at 24.13 with 15 innings in 14 matches. His batting was improving as his effectiveness as a bowler declined slightly. There were no five wicket hauls this summer, and he bowled 502.1 overs to take 48 wickets at an average of 15.62.

The first Players v Gentlemen match, played at the Kennington Oval on 26, 27 and 28 June, ended in the first drawn match between them since 1839, with the Players needing 33 to win with two wickets in hand when stumps were drawn. Recent heavy rain had meant a dead pitch, and bowlers of Jackson's pace could not get the ball to rise more than half-stump high which made life easy for the batsmen. Jackson started well, taking two early wickets in the Gentlemen's first innings, beating E.B.Rowley and H.M.Marshall for pace and bowling them for 6 and 0 respectively. As the wicket eased John Walker hit up 98 and F.P.Miller made 51 with the total reaching 276, Jackson finishing with two for 40 in 23 overs. Tom Hayward scored 77 and Jackson a hard-hit 35 as the Players finished with 244. The Gentlemen scored 211 (C.G.Lyttleton 57) in their second innings which left the Players needing 244 to win. Steady batting took them to 211 for eight, but time called a halt to what would clearly have been an exciting finish.

For the Lord's match which began on 14 July, selection of the teams was limited to those under 30 years of age. The idea was to try to even the balance between the teams as the Gentlemen had not beaten the Players since 1853, and it was felt that one of the reasons was that their players, being amateurs, abandoned the game for a more profitable career earlier than the professionals did. On this occasion the change made no difference at all as the Players won by 157 runs, scoring 110 and 246. The Gentlemen made 130 and 69 with Jackson taking nought for 29 in 18 overs.

There was only one clash between the two great professional Elevens and it took place at Lord's on 9, 10 and 11 June, with the AEE triumphing by four wickets. £214.9s was raised for the benefit of the Cricketers Fund. Jackson took four wickets for 87 in 48 overs in the match as the UAEE scored 126 and 129 in their two innings. The AEE made 203 and were set only 53 to win. After collapsing to 14 for six they were seen home by A.Clarke and G.Anderson without further alarms.

Nottinghamshire played home and away matches against Cambridgeshire and Surrey. At the Fenner's Ground on 6, 7 June, (it should have started on 5 June, but rain washed out the first day), Jackson was the batting star for Nottinghamshire with innings of 28* and 37* in a low-scoring encounter in the County's totals of 100 and 145 for seven. He bowled 90 overs, 52 unchanged in the first innings, as Cambridgeshire were bowled out for 96 and 148. Jackson took four wickets for 105 in the match as Nottinghamshire won the match by three wickets. The return match at Trent Bridge on 3 and 4 July was easily won by the Midland County by an innings and 39 runs. Nottinghamshire scored 231 and R.C.Tinley starred with the ball, taking fifteen for 78 with his underhand lobs whereas Jackson bowled only 8 overs, taking one for 4 as the Cambridgeshire innings totalled 45 and 147. As the match had finished early, a single wicket match was arranged between Jackson, R.Daft and Clarke for Nottinghamshire, and Tarrant, Hayward and Carpenter for Cambridgeshire. Jackson brushed aside the Cambridge trio for 1 run between them. The Nottinghamshire three mustered a total of 12, but no second innings was possible as rain washed out the remaining time.

The Oval fixture against Surrey was played in dreadful weather on 13 and 14 June. Jackson starred as a batsman scoring 59 in the Nottinghamshire innings of 172 after which he took three for 11 in Surrey's 108. In reply Nottinghamshire were seven for no wicket when the rains came and caused an abandonment. At Trent Bridge on 28, 29 and 30 July Nottinghamshire won by five wickets. Jackson took five wickets for 89 in 40 overs in this match, with Surrey scoring 133 and 187, and Nottinghamshire 224 and 99 for five.

The first North v South fixture of the season took place at Old Trafford on 29, 30 and 31 May. Scheduled for three days, it was left unfinished when the second day was rained off. Jackson took four for 42 in 33.1 overs in the South's first innings, and three for 33 in the second. The South scored 127 and 137, batting one short in their second innings as Caffyn had an injured knee. In the return match at Lord's, which began on 21 July and was played as a benefit match for Jem Grundy, Richard Daft hit a brilliant 118 for the North, and F.W.Wright made 50 as they totalled 271. George Tarrant had a fine spell of eight for 26 in 23.2 overs as the South were dismissed for 61, and although they did better in the second innings, making 200, the North still won by an innings and 10 runs. Jackson, only required in the second innings, took two for 18 in the match.

Nottinghamshire 1862.
Standing (l to r): R.Daft, J.Grundy, G.Parr, G.Anderson,(Umpire), J.Jackson, C.Brampton, A.E.Bateman, J.Johnson (Hon.Secretary), G.Wootton, A.Clarke.
On ground: R.C.Tinley, C.F.Daft, S.Biddulph.
[Roger Mann Collection]

On 5 and 6 August the North played Surrey at the Oval and beat them by ten wickets. Jackson took three for 31 as Surrey were bowled out for 151. Carpenter hit 91* for the North and George Anderson 56, but things were evenly poised at 149 for eight until R.C.Tinley arrived at the crease as tenth man in and hit up 56 to help Carpenter take the score to 242. The eventual total was 266 and Surrey were rolled over for 121 in their second innings (Jackson nought for 30). In the return which was played at Salford on 14 and 15 August, Surrey scored 156 and 83, with Jackson taking four wickets for 68 in the match in 48 overs. The North led by 27 on the first innings with Tom Hayward scoring 54 and they needed only 57 to win, but F.P.Miller and G.Griffith bowled so well that getting the runs took them 60 overs. At one stage Hayward and Parr took 90 minutes to take the score from 10 to 26, and the North had been reduced to 46 for nine when Tinley joined John Jackson, and the pair carried them to victory by one wicket, Jackson finishing with 13* and Tinley 9*.

Kent had not played an eleven-a-side match against England since 1853, but they played one on 30 June and 1 July at Lord's. It did not seem a good idea as they lost by an innings and 23 runs. Jackson had a burst of three for 16 in 18 overs in Kent's first innings of 82 but bowled only 5 overs in the second, dismissing the opening batsman, W.H.Fryer, in taking one for 5 as Kent made 99 all out. England totalled 204. A lesson having been learned, Kent played with 14 men at Canterbury on 11 and 12 August and won by 170 runs. England was not at full strength as stars like Hayward, Daft, Anderson, H.Stephenson, Lockyer and Mortlock were all unavailable for various reasons, and Carpenter received a blow on the elbow from a ball by R.Lipscomb which rendered him incapable of continuing. Kent made 171 and 236, England scoring 105 and 132. Jackson made 44 (run out) in England's second innings, batting for a while with E.M.Grace who scored 56. In Kent's first innings he took four for 47 in 31 overs, 0/17 in second innings.

The most sensational event of the season took place at The Oval when England met Surrey on 25, 26 and 27 August. England began by scoring 503, the highest score made in a first-class match to that date. They batted for nine hours, 55 minutes with Hayward hitting 117, Grundy 95 and Parr 94. But the real sensations began when John Lillywhite, one of the umpires, took exception to the bowling action of Edgar Willsher and refused to change his verdict that the bowler's standard delivery was unfair. Bowlers were supposed to deliver with the arm below the level of the shoulder, and Lillywhite claimed that Willsher did not comply with this. The only solution to the impasse was for another umpire, G.Street, to replace Lillywhite on the third day when Surrey made 102 (Jackson three for 19 in 17 overs) and 154 for six (Jackson two for 42). The action of Lillywhite eventually led to a change in the law, allowing freedom to bowlers to deliver the ball from above shoulder height.

John Jackson appeared in 26 of the AEE matches in 1862, 15 of which were won, scoring 263 runs and taking 289 wickets in a mammoth stint of 1257 overs between 15 May and 4 October with hardly a break. Many of the games took place in the North of England, especially in Yorkshire with some other excursions into Lincolnshire, Surrey and Hampshire along the way.

The first match was at Kinning Park, Glasgow on 15, 16 and 17 May when the AEE played out a draw with XXII of the Clydesdale Club, Jackson taking eight for 23 in 24 overs in the locals' second innings. The next match was against XXII of the Sheffield York Club at the Endcliffe Ground, Sheffield on 19, 20 and 21 May. Jackson took a fine twelve for 19 in the first innings in a four wicket win followed by three for 22 in the second innings. The pitch was a rough one, newly laid with cinders working through the ground in places, making it rough and dangerous on which to be facing a bowler of Jackson's pace, and he made full use of the conditions. The Sheffield Club were bowled out for 46, with the young players in the side succumbing to his magnificent bowling which all present agreed was as fine a specimen of cricket as had been played anywhere. A crowd of 4,000 watched the second day's play, and takings over the three days were £108.9s.11d. The band of the 41st Regiment was also in attendance. The AEE were set 75 to win, and Jackson helped things along with a brisk 17 after being dropped off the first ball.

The next game, which was played on 22, 23 and 24 May, brought a win by eight wickets over a XXII of Rossall School. Jackson decimated the opposition, taking seven for 15 and eleven for 33 in 57.3 overs. This was despite the boys having the assistance of two or three Old Rossallians and three professionals.

On 22 May the AEE began a three day match against XX of Yorkshire at the Clarence Ground, Barnsley, winning by 27 runs. The match clashed with the Surrey v Yorkshire game at The Oval, so some of the best Yorkshire players were not available. Jackson took eight for 44 and five for 17 in a total of 81 overs. A large banner depicting a crown and the motto 'God Save the Queen' hung over the entrance gate, and a goodly crowd enjoyed the carnival occasion and the refreshments provided. John Thewlis, a future Yorkshire captain, played in this match, top scoring in both innings with 38 and 12, and being presented with a new bat.

Jackson's next match for the AEE was on 2, 3 and 4 June against XXII of Southampton Union Club which the Eleven lost by 67 runs. Jackson, perhaps tired after a long journey, bowled only in the second innings when he took four for 42 in 35 overs. A crowd of 1,600 paid for admission to the match. His next game for AEE was at Christchurch Ground in Oxford on 16, 17 and 18 June against XVI Undergraduates, where he took part in a 'tied' match. Oxford scored 92 and 57, AEE making 53 and 96. Jackson took ten for 42 and seven for 21 in a total of 77 overs. Interestingly, John Thewlis played in this match for the AEE.

A three day match against XVIII of Manchester Broughton at Salford on 19 June was turned into a one day match by rain. The AEE made 225. Jackson dismissed both the Club openers, reducing them to twelve for 2, but that was where the game ended. A match against XXIII of Lincolnshire on 23, 24 and 25 June on the Lindum Club ground was won by 87 runs, with Jackson bowling 15 overs and taking two for 16. An interesting footnote in the local paper says that one Lincoln player walked the 18 miles from Sleaford to take part in the match, having missed the team coach. He arrived just in time to bat at the fall of the twentieth wicket.

On 10 July Jackson played against XXII of Morley in a drawn match in which he bowled 82 overs and took eight for 87. Morley needed one run to win with three wickets left when the game ended. At Grantham a week later the AEE faced H.Handley's XXII. After following on, Handley's side hit up 168 in their second innings (Jackson five for 21). AEE needed 88 to win and struggled to get them. At 82 for nine, John Jackson strode out to join George Parr, and the two Notts men saw their side home by one wicket.

On 24 and 25 July at Barton Court, Kintbury in Berkshire, the AEE were well beaten by seventeen wickets by Captain Handley's XXII. On what was clearly a bad wicket the AEE made 38 and 54, and the XXII scored 64 and 30 for four. Jackson took twelve for 21 and four for 13 in 43 overs in the match. On 31 July, on Parr and Wisden's ground at Leamington Spa, the AEE lost a match against XVI of the Free Foresters by two wickets. Jackson had two Herculean bowling stints – 55 overs to take six for 68 in the first innings and 35.1 to take five for 48 in the second.

A defeat followed on 7, 8 and 9 August at Doncaster where XXII of South

Yorkshire beat the AEE by 90 runs. In the locals' first innings Jackson took three for 6 in 16 overs, and he had another prodigious spell of 42 overs to take twelve for 24 in the second, but the AEE were skittled out by the two professional given men, I.Hodgson and W.Slinn, for totals of 62 and 23. The match against XXII of the Sheffield (Shrewsbury) Club on 18, 19 and 20 August at Bramall Lane was won by five wickets, with Jackson putting in a bowling marathon of 48 consecutive overs in the first innings to take nine wickets for 19, and 27 overs in the second to take one for 20. R.C.Tinley took twenty-six wickets for 92 in the match with his lobs.

Tinley starred once again against XXII of The Royal Artillery at Woolwich on 21, 22 and 23 August, taking twenty-one wickets for 115 runs. Jackson helped out with nine for 39 as the AEE won by six wickets.

The AEE made another 'missionary' call when they went to Southsea in Hampshire on 28 August to play against XXII of the East Hants Club before a good crowd of paying customers. The AEE made only 84 and 61 in their innings, but Jackson took twelve for 49 in 27 overs in East Hants 105 all out in their first innings, and, with his bowling partner, George Tarrant, reducing the locals to 43 for ten, the margin of victory being eleven wickets.

Immediately after the match the AEE had to hurry off to catch the 3.00 pm train to Bradford where their next match was due to take place. They may not have been too upset that, after a long journey, the start of the match against XVIII of Bradford was delayed by rain until 1.00 pm. The third day was completely washed out, with Jackson bowling only 7 overs on what must have been a dead wicket after all the rain.

On 4 September the AEE began a match against XXII of Leicestershire at Hon.H.A.Reynolds-.Moreton's ground at Lindridge House near Desford and won by 91 runs, with Jackson bowling 34 overs in each innings and returning figures of seven for 19 and six for 30.

Jackson was beginning a purple patch which was to see him take another 101 wickets before the end of the season. At Bishop's Stortford on 8, 9 and 10 September he took four for 11 in the second innings in 24 overs, as the AEE won by 130 runs. The local people made a real carnival of the event, with 6,000 paying for admission over the three days and the band of the 17th East Essex Rifles entertaining the crowd during the intervals. The AEE had to rush to catch the 5.22 pm train to Huddersfield where they were due to play XXII Yorkshire Colts at 11.00 am next day at Lascelles Hall - such were the stresses of the long distance travelling the AEE had to undertake. After Huddersfield they were due to play at Godalming in Surrey before returning to Batley near Huddersfield for the match after that. One does wonder whether the fixtures could have been better planned.

In the match against Yorkshire Colts Jackson bowled 58 overs, taking eight for 28 and three for 39 as the AEE won by four wickets. Against XXII of Godalming on 15, 16 and 17 September he took eight for 18 and ten for 27 in a two wicket win. Back in Yorkshire, at Batley on 18, 19 and 20 September, the AEE made 84 and, and then Jackson and Willsher knocked over the first five local men for no runs, just five of the 24 ducks recorded by Batley players in their two innings. The AEE won the match by 62 runs with Jackson finishing nine for 23 and four for 19 after bowling 26 overs in each innings. He did not bowl at all against Sheffield Collegiate at Bramall Lane

On 25 September the AEE played a XXII of Scarborough, losing by 39 runs. One of the club's given professional bowlers, W.Slinn, took all ten wickets in one AEE innings for 23 and sixteen for 42 in the match. Jackson took twenty of the Scarborough wickets (nine for 16 and eleven for 15) in a total of 75 overs, but it was low scoring by the AEE batsmen that cost them the game. They made only 47 and 32 despite Scarborough being bowled out for 23 in their second innings - there were 13 ducks and the highest score was made by a given man, E.Stephenson, with 13.

The AEE beat XXII of Harrogate by an innings and 65 runs in a match starting on 29 September - there was no talk of having to play too much cricket in those days! Jackson took twenty-two wickets for 44 runs in the match in 56 overs. The side's last match was at the Royal Park Ground, Woodhouse, near Leeds, where Jackson took twenty wickets for 27, bowling another 62 overs in the process. The AEE won by seven wickets and on 4 October could finally have a break from cricket and travelling.

Jackson took part in ten first-class games in 1863. He proved his growing batting ability by hitting a century for Nottinghamshire against Kent at Cranbrook. He bowled 470.3 overs and took 58 wickets at an average of 11.48. His best figures were the seven for 48 he took for the AEE against the UAEE and he also took twelve wickets for 43 for Nottinghamshire against Kent in the same match in which he scored 100, a match-winning all-round performance if ever there was one.

Jackson did not play in the Players v Gentlemen match at The Oval. Indeed, only T.Hearne and E.Willsher appeared for the Players in both the Lord's and Oval matches. In the Lord's match which began on 29 June, the professionals completed their usual win over the amateurs, beating them by eight wickets. Hayward made a fine 112* in the Players' 231 all out after which Jackson and Tarrant got amongst the Gentlemen's batting and bowled them out for 119 and 126. Jackson bowled 50 overs in the match, taking four for 34 and five for 41. Tarrant took five for 67 and three for 54, with the pair bowling throughout both innings apart from a token contribution of six overs from G.Wootton. The Hon. C.G.Lyttleton, who top-scored with 29 in the Gentlemen's first innings, considered that Jackson was the best fast bowler of his time The Players got the nine runs they needed to win for the loss of two wickets.

The match between the AEE and the UAEE began at Lord's on 25 May on a fiery wicket and resulted in a grim struggle with the bowlers always on top. The ground was parched and totally unprepared after a drought, a new pitch having to be cut after the match umpires deemed that no play was possible on the one originally selected. Amongst its various defects it had a large hole immediately in front of it. The start was delayed until 12.30 pm whilst the new pitch was got ready, and play began with 6,000 people present. The ball was coming through at various heights, and Jackson and Willsher soon dismissed the first five batsmen for 16 runs. The batsmen were not the only ones having problems as the wicketkeeper, H.H.Stephenson, was poleaxed by a Jackson delivery which kicked terrifyingly off the pitch, and prudently retired to a safer distance. A recovery of sorts took the UAEE score to 109, bolstered by some 20 byes given away by some fumbling at long stop. Jackson finished with seven for 48 in 25 overs. *The Times* described the pitch as 'very bumptious with the ball sometimes rearing head high or rattling about the batsmen's ribs and hands and sometimes shooting along the treacherous ground'. It sounds like a typical Lord's wicket of the time! Things got no better when the AEE batted, with only Hayward staying long and making 30 out of 92 all out. T.Hearne hit 44 and Carpenter 24 as the UAEE scored 150 in their second innings, Jackson taking one for 23. Needing 168 to win, the AEE could only make 97 and lost by 70 runs.

Jackson's county side, Nottinghamshire, played Yorkshire for the first time in 1863 with the inaugural match taking place at the Great Horton Road ground in Bradford on 22, 23 and 24 June. Yorkshire won by eight wickets with Jackson taking three for 48 in 41 overs in Yorkshire's first innings of 144, and one for 23 in the 73 for two they needed to win in their second innings. Nottinghamshire totalled 128 and 88. In the return match at Trent Bridge on 9 July, Nottinghamshire gained revenge, winning by 6 runs after Yorkshire had scored 243. Jackson for once went wicketless, taking nought for 65 in 32 overs. Nottinghamshire batted steadily to make 162 and 181 with no batsman scoring more than 42 but nine passing 20. Yorkshire needed 101 to win but were bowled out for 93 with Jackson taking two for 32 in 32 overs. The real hero for Nottinghamshire was Jem Grundy who took five for 13 in 23 overs.

On 11, 12 and 13 June Nottinghamshire played Kent at Trent Bridge in a match drawn in Nottinghamshire's favour. Jackson bowled 22 overs in Kent's first innings of 109, taking four for 43. The return match at Swift Park, Cranbrook on 23 and 24 July saw Jackson and Grundy bowling unchanged to dismiss Kent for 58 and 45, with Jackson taking six for 23 and six for 40 in a total of 63.3 overs. Nottinghamshire were in trouble themselves at 61 for six when Jackson came in to bat. Powerful stroke play quickly took the match away from Kent and Jackson hit his maiden century, finishing with exactly 100, R.C.Tinley helping with 63 as Nottinghamshire finished on 280 and won by an innings and 177 runs.

The first of the North v South clashes was arranged by the Manchester Club and was played at Old Trafford on 21, 22 and 23 May. On the first day the South made 157 (H.Stephenson 60, Jackson nought for 44), and the North replied with 86 for five. Jackson batted well for 35 before being torpedoed by a shooter from Willsher. On the second day the total reached 286. The South scored 185 with E.M.Grace getting 43 and Jackson taking four for 54 in 32 overs. The North now needed 58 to win. Jackson opened the batting and taking an immediate liking to the bowling, hit an unbeaten 41 as the

North won by ten wickets.

At Lord's on 20, 21 and 22 July the North triumphed again by 29 runs but Jackson bowled only 10 overs, taking nought for 32. A third encounter took place at the Wavertree Road Ground, Edge Hill, Liverpool, on 27, 28 and 29 August, and again the North won, this time by 84 runs. Jackson bowled E.M.Grace for nought in the second innings whilst taking ten for 85 in 60 overs in the match which was a low- scoring affair, with the North making 114 and 146 and the South 115 and 61.

Jackson's other first-class appearance was at Lord's on 6, 7 July when an England XI defeated XXIII of Kent by an innings and five runs. E.M.Grace scored 52, Griffith 43 and Carpenter and Parr both passed 30 as England made 230 all out. Tarrant took sixteen wickets including ten for 40 in the Kent second innings, and Jackson took five for 51 in 38 overs to complete the destruction.

Jackson took part in 24 matches against odds for the AEE, batting 40 times with ten not outs and scoring 258 runs at an average of 8.60. He took 255 wickets and 30 catches.

This year's trail began on 4, 5 and 6 May at Pudsey near Leeds, the future birthplace of Herbert Sutcliffe, Len Hutton and others. Nobody of this class was playing in the local XXII, but the AEE struggled to win by 7 runs with Jackson taking nine wickets in Pudsey's first innings. The next game was on 11, 12 and 13 May at Bramall Lane against XVIII of Sheffield and was played as a benefit match for the well-known Sheffield professional, William Slinn. Rain ruined the first day and the match was drawn. Jackson took only two wickets in the match whilst R.C.Tinley took fourteen with his lobs. On 14, 15 and 16 May the side went up to Glasgow and played XXII of the Clydesdale Club at Kinning Park. In a tight finish the local side, set 63 to win, ended up on 56 for seventeen wickets, Jackson having taken eleven of them to supplement the five he had taken in the Glasgow Club's first innings.

The AEE returned to Yorkshire where they beat XXII of Bradford, Birkenshaw and District by 30 runs at Birkenshaw near Leeds on 18, 19 and 20 May. Jackson took nine wickets in each innings, and it is a tribute to his accuracy that 12 men were bowled and one was lbw. Jackson's next match for the AEE on 28, 29 and 30 May brought him face to face with the 14 year-old W.G.Grace who was playing for XXII of the Lansdown Club at the Sydenham Field in Bath. Grace was unlucky enough to make a pair, dismissed twice by R.C.Tinley, but his elder brother, E.M., scored 73 as Lansdown led by 30 runs on first innings. Tinley and Tarrant hit back, taking sixteen wickets between them to tumble the locals out for 57 in their second innings, leaving the AEE to make 88 to win which they did for the loss of three wickets.

On 1 June the AEE began a match on the Trinity Cricket Ground against a Halifax and District XXII. Haygarth commented that 'the Halifax District must be very large since many of their players come from Sheffield, Bradford and Leeds'. The local paper describes grumbling amongst the crowd that the team selection had favoured 'outsiders' before local men. The XXII won by 54 runs. Jackson, batting at No. 9, came in at 88 for seven and hit up 37, with some brilliant hitting. He also took nine wickets in the match. E.Stephenson hit 82 for the Halifax side but, as he had already faced the AEE on behalf of XVIII of Sheffield, this perfectly illustrates what Haygarth and the local crowd were concerned about. Some 8,000 to 10,000 spectators watched the three days play, with the Halifax ladies in their finery adding beauty and lustre to the scene. The band of the West Yorkshire Rifles played music during the luncheon interval. The police had to eject some rowdy members of the crowd who were trying to watch the game without paying admission money

At Old Trafford on 4 June Jackson took three wickets in a drawn match with XVIII of Manchester Broughton Club. A lengthy trip down to Southampton to play XXII of Southampton Union on 8, 9, and 10 June saw the AEE win by 65 run, with Jackson taking nineteen wickets thus avenging their 1862 defeat at the same venue. The *Southampton Times* spoke of the enormous interest generated by the match, with immense crowds attending despite the often threatening weather. The paper recorded that the long-stopping of Mr Lucas for Southampton with great admiration. Jackson bowled ten of his second innings victims.

At Earlsheaton near Dewsbury on 15, 16 and 17 June the XXII were supplemented by the likes of E.Stephenson of Sheffield and I.Hodgson of Bradford. Stephenson top-scored with 46 and Hodgson took ten wickets, the assistance from outsiders materially assisting Dewsbury's innings win. Jackson took seven wickets in Dewsbury's only innings. In the next AEE match at Salford against XVIII of Manchester Broughton on 18, 19 and 20 June he took nine wickets in each innings of the local XVIII as the AEE won by four wickets.

The local paper at Redditch, the town where the AEE played their next match on 25 June against XXII of Redditch, gave the match blanket coverage, labelling it one of the 'events' in the history of the town. Over 1,000 people attended each day's play and the Rifle Corps band was there to keep the crowd entertained. One shilling was charged for admission and a tastefully erected evergreen entrance was surmounted by the motto 'Success to Cricket'. Jackson took 12 wickets and Hayward scored an unbeaten 71 for the AEE with the bowling of Jackson being likened to 'a strong-arm pounding at the walls'. The second AEE innings lasted until 6.00 pm on the third day and the Redditch XXII were 17 for seven (Jackson two wickets) when the match ended.

2, 3 and 4 July saw the AEE back in Yorkshire playing XXII of Morley and District who were defeated by 6 runs. Jackson took 13 wickets and was top scorer with 36 in the AEE second innings. There was a dispute in this match as to whether a hit by J.Rowbotham should count as a six. He hit the ball through the main entrance gate on to the road where a passer-by stopped it. After a heated discussion in which the local umpire insisted that such a hit should only count three, it was agreed that six was more appropriate.

Jackson's next game for the AEE was at Basingstoke on 16 July where XXII of Basingstoke were defeated by an innings and 125 runs with Jackson taking 14 wickets although in *S&B* Volume VIII Haygarth stressed that there were a number of different versions of the scorecard which led him on to one of his many complaints about scoring standards – 'the carelessness of scorers generally is to be deplored by all cricketers.... Careless scoring is continued up to the present time, those employed evidently not being under proper supervision.'

At the Chuckery Ground, Walsall the AEE beat XXII of Walsall by 11 runs in a match which began on 27 July and was notable for the performance of W.H.Moore of Walsall hitting a century against an attack consisting of Jackson, Tarrant, Willsher, Tinley and Hayward – no mean feat! Prior to this only one other batsman had hit a hundred for a local side against a professional eleven. Apart from J.Brown who made 21 no one else in the Walsall team got into double figures. Moore was given an enthusiastic reception by the 3,000 strong crowd. Jackson took only two wickets in the match, but was top scorer for the AEE with 49.

The next match was against XXII of Longsight on 30 and 31 July. The AEE won by ten wickets with Jackson picking up ten wickets in the first innings before moving on to Boston Spa on 3, 4 and 5 August where the local XXII was defeated by an innings and 23 runs, Jackson taking four wickets. Haygarth made the point that so many of the best Yorkshire players were engaged by the local side that the match could reasonably have been designated AEE v Yorkshire.

On 6, 7 and 8 August the AEE was in action against XXII of Ashton-under-Lyne, winning by two wickets. Jackson had an eight wicket haul. Joseph Rowbotham steered the AEE to victory with an unbeaten 31. This match was followed by a break of just over a week after which the AEE was in action again against XXII of Lawton Hall or Cheshire. Jackson took 17 wickets and once again Haygarth complained about 'serious scoring errors'.

Moving on to Harrogate on 20, 21 and 22 August the AEE met XXII of Harrogate and won by 29 runs, Jackson added a further ten wickets to his tally. This was followed by a match on 24, 25 and 26 August against XXII of Scarborough who had the assistance of several given men. The AEE was dismissed for 59 and the XXII reached 132 with Jackson taking nine for 33. In their second innings the AEE made 149 thus leaving Scarborough 77 to win but Jackson took eleven for 26 and Scarborough lost by ten runs. The Castle Ground was packed and excursion trains brought spectators into the town each morning.

On 31 August and 1 September the AEE played XXII of Bristol and District at Durdham Downs in Clifton. The local team did not have the assistance of any professionals. E.M.Grace opened the batting for the locals and the 15 year-old W.G.Grace was also in the team as well as H and A.Grace. A crowd of 3,000 on the first day saw E.M.Grace – one of Jackson's eight victims - make 87 while W.G. in his first full season made 32. Bristol were too strong for the AEE who lost by an innings and 20 runs.

Jackson's next game for the AEE was on 7, 8 and 9 September against XXII of Hull at the Kingston Ground. The match was won by six wickets with Jackson taking three wickets. The match was interrupted by a hurricane which blew down many of the tents erected for the occasion.

At York on 10 September the match against XXII of York and District attracted numerous spectators and the Band of the 16th Lancers was present. On a ground, made heavy by recent rain, the York team missed several catches, but the long-stopping of Stott drew regular applause. In those days long-stop was a very important fielding position, reducing the number of byes conceded on rough wickets by wicket-keepers. Jackson took 12 wickets and the AEE won by 83 runs.

The final match of the season was at Royal Park, Leeds against a local XXII. Jackson took 11 wickets in a drawn game and E.M.Grace distinguished himself by taking seven catches. We should mention a match in which Jackson played as a given man for his home town of Retford against the AEE on 3, 4 and 5 September as among his victims were E.M.Grace, T.Hayward, H.H.Stephenson, G.Tarrant and Julius Caesar.

Jackson's season began as early as 6 April with a match for Nottinghamshire against XXII Nottinghamshire Colts in which he took nine for 9 in the first innings followed by another three in the second innings. In a return match on 28 and 29 September he took four for 27 and ten for 18 in another rain-ruined match. He also played for Nottinghamshire against XIV Free Foresters at Trent Bridge on 13, 14 and 15 August in a match which ended in a tie.

Chapter Eight

The England Eleven in Australia and New Zealand 1863/64

John Jackson would not have had much time to visit Mahala and his growing family before he was off on his travels again. This time he was heading for Liverpool to join his England colleagues for a tour of Australia and New Zealand, Captained by George Parr of Nottinghamshire, the team comprised Julius Caesar, Caffyn and T.Lockyer of Surrey, R.Carpenter, T.Hayward and G.Tarrant from Cambridgeshire, A.Clarke, R.C.Tinley and J.Jackson from Nottinghamshire, G.Anderson, from Yorkshire and the amateur E.M.Grace from Gloucestershire. A dinner was held in the team's honour at the Adelphi Hotel in Liverpool on 14 October and the following day they set out on the *SS Great Britain* for Melbourne which they reached on 16 December.

There was a fairly leisurely start to the tour as the first match was not played until 1 January 1864. The return voyage began on 26 April and the team eventually arrived back in England on 13 June after an absence of almost eight months.

The opening match was in Melbourne against XXII of Victoria and was played in front of a truly gigantic crowd with 40,000 paying for admission. T.W.Wills was selected to play for Victoria but, having travelled 1800 miles from North Queensland, he arrived too late to take part. Jackson took six for 48 in 33 overs in Victoria's first innings of 146 and four for 18 in their second innings of 143. England replied with 176 with Hayward making 61 and Carpenter 59. England needed 114 to win but finished nine runs short with six wickets in hand.

The team's first win came on a dreadful ground, devoid of grass, at Sandhurst, where XXII of Bendigo were beaten on 7, 8 and 9 January by 144 runs. Jackson, a truly frightening proposition on such a rough wicket, had match figures of thirteen for 22 in 43 overs. Only two Bendigo batsmen reached double figures and the second innings top scorer made 5.

On 11, 12 and 13 January XXII of Ballarat were beaten by an innings and 12 runs with Jackson taking three for 23 in 15 overs. This was followed by seven for 11 against XXII of Ararat who were dismissed for 35 and 34. This was the match in which Tinley took twenty-six for 45. Tinley followed this up with twenty-one wickets against XXII of Maryborough. Jackson only bowled in the second Maryborough innings, taking six for 5 in 24 overs.

Having beaten everyone except Victoria by wide margins, the English team sailed for New Zealand on 25 January aboard the *SS Alhambra,* heading for Port Chalmers in New Zealand where they were due to spend a month before returning to Australia. Before mentioning the cricket we must take note of an incident that occurred when here the team attended a Maori gathering. A leading Maori lady offered the kiss of greeting to a member of the team. George Parr suggested that John Jackson should step forward to do the honours as he was part gypsy. Jackson, however, refused the invitation and Parr kissed the lady himself so everyone was satisfied.

The first match was at Dunedin on 2, 3 and 4 February which was reached in a coach and six driven by the well-known coachman, Cabbage-Tree Ned. Otago were beaten by nine wickets. Haygarth commented that the 'ground was a wretched one, which had only just been laid, and was in no way fit for cricket.' Part of the game was played on a fresh pitch, nearly at right angles with the original one. Jackson bowled 70.1 overs, 43 maidens and took eleven wickets for 42 in the match. Hayward took twenty-four wickets for 70. Otago made 71 and 83; England 99 and 58 for one. It was certainly a poor pitch on which to bat!

After this match the Eleven played a combined XXII of Canterbury and Otago who were dismissed for 91 and 66 with England making 73 (Grace 42) in reply. Tinley took twenty-five wickets and Lockyer stumped nine and caught three batsmen, with Carpenter taking seven catches. An unusual scorecard entry is recorded for a batsman named Powys of the combined team: the entry reads, 'Left the wicket thinking he was out'. Jackson took two wickets in the match.

The next match on 8 and 9 February was against XXII of Christchurch, a game the England team won by an innings and 2 runs. In their first innings Christchurch made 30 with Jackson (six for 11) and Tinley (thirteen for 18) proving irresistible. After the match ended Parr led a team consisting of six of the England side with five local men against a similar combination captained by George Anderson. Parr's side won by 7 runs, and Jackson, who played on Anderson's side, did not bowl.

On 16, 17 and 18 February the England team met XXII of Otago at Dunedin, winning by an innings and 51 runs. Jackson bowled 45 overs with 32 maidens and took ten for 21 in Otago's first innings, taking seven more wickets when Otago went in again. After this match several foot races took place with Jackson beating Tinley in a 100 yards race before losing to Caffyn over the same distance. Grace won the competition for throwing the cricket ball, hurling a throw 101 yards. The Eleven then planted some trees in commemoration of their visit before heading back to Australia where they arrived on 27 February.

In their first match back in Australia – 2, 3 and 4 March - the team played at Campbell's Creek against XXII of Castlemaine, winning quite easily by an innings and 37 runs. Jackson took four for 11 in the first innings and did not bowl in the second when the bowling was done by Tinley (twelve for 28) and Hayward (eight for 13). Carpenter took eight catches. Haygarth comments that 'The Castlemaine XXII were all bona fide residents of the district'. Some sterling resistance was offered by one of the local batsmen,

George Parr's Team in Australia and New Zealand 1863/64.
[Nottinghamshire CCC]

a man named Easton, who batted for more than two hours for 3 runs, a feat of stonewalling to rank with the very best. After this match Jackson and Grace played a single wicket match against a Castlemaine XI. Grace scored 13, Jackson 0, with one extra, after which Jackson dismissed all eleven locals for 2 runs between them, bowling nine and causing the other two to hit their own wickets.

The next match was the sole first-class match played on the tour, and it involved a side of six English players captained by George Parr plus five local men, against a side captained by George Anderson of similar make-up. Jackson played in Anderson's team which won by four wickets with Tom Lockyer playing the decisive innings, scoring 44 and 40*. Parr's side made 153 and 129, Jackson taking three for 77 in the match. Anderson's side scored 168 and 115 for six. This match was played at Melbourne between 6 and 9 March after which the team sailed to Sydney on the steamship *Alexandra*, arriving there on 14 March.

The first match in New South Wales was played at Domain against XXII of New South Wales on 16, 17 and 18 March, although the match actually ended on 24 March as all the days between 18 and 23 were washed out by rain. The Governor of the Colony attended the match which England won by four wickets. Jackson put in a long shift, bowling a total of 68.2 overs in the game to take five for 15 and nine for 20, with Haygarth noting once again that different versions of the individual scores and dismissals existed in other publications. The second match at Domain on 26, 28 and 29 March was also seriously interrupted by rain with only one innings a side being finished. New South Wales made 102 and 3 for one wicket, with England scoring 114. Jackson took five for 25 in 30 overs. The third game against New South Wales was much closer, with England only winning by one wicket. It was a low- scoring match with the locals making 68 (Jackson seven for 21 in 47 overs) and 83 (Jackson nought for 9). England scores were 75 and 77 for nine. Tarrant had taken six wickets for no runs in 8.3 overs in the New South Wales first innings.

The team next played XXII of Geelong and the match should have started on 11 April, but was reduced to a two day affair owing to the late arrival of the tourists. The game was drawn with Jackson taking six wickets. An additional match between Elevens, again led by Anderson and Parr, was played on 14 and 15 April at Maryborough and was won by Anderson's side by 56 runs. Jackson played in Parr's team, taking three for 68 in 47.2 overs. He also made the highest score in the match, scoring 45 as an opener in Parr's side's first innings.

The team met XXII of Ballarat on 18, 19 and 20 April where Carpenter hit the only hundred of the tour, scoring 121 in nine hours, while Parr scored 65 in a total of 310. Ballarat scored 128 (Jackson six for 15 in 24 overs) and were 48 for fifteen wickets (Jackson two for 6 in 12 overs) when time was called. Tinley's lobs had accounted for seventeen wickets in this game.

It must be mentioned that the English fast bowlers, Jackson and Tarrant, were storing up a lot of grief for England whilst in New South Wales. An interested spectator at their net practices was a lad named F.R.Spofforth, the 'Demon' himself, who was to take fourteen wickets for 90 at the Kennington Oval in 1882 when Australia won a Test Match in England for the first time, a feat that led to the inauguration of 'The Ashes' series.

The team's last match in Australia was in Melbourne on 21, 22 and 23 April when more bad weather was experienced, with the wicket having to be changed for each new innings. XXII of Victoria made 150 with Jackson bowling 37 overs, 19 maidens and taking ten for 34. England replied with 131, and Victoria were 83 for seventeen wickets when the match was abandoned. Jackson took two for 31 in 25.3 overs.

Jackson took part in eighteen matches, batting 23 times, scoring 214 runs at an average of 12.58. He took 139 wickets and held 22 catches so it was a successful trip for him and he more than maintained his reputation.

With the exception of Caffyn, who had accepted a coaching job in Australia, and E.M.Grace, the rest of the side, all of whom cleared about £250 each after expenses, embarked on the Bombay steamer for England, arriving at Dover on 13 June. The 1864 English season was by then under way.

Jackson holding a cricket ball:
in his hands an Instrument of terror and destruction.
[Roger Mann Collection]

Chapter Nine

Still at the Top

John Jackson had missed the start of the season and he now spent two weeks at home in Retford with his family who may well have forgotten what he looked like! His first match of the new season was for the Players against the Gentlemen at Lord's on 27 and 28 June, a game in which eight of the English party that had toured Australia appeared in the Players' side. The Players made 187 with W.Mortlock of Surrey hitting 71, and this score was enough to win the match by an innings and 68 runs. Jackson's bowling was surplus to requirements as the Gentlemen were skittled out for 60 and 59 by Tarrant and Willsher, who bowled unchanged in both innings. The Gentlemen batted for only 90 minutes in the first innings and 65 in the second. This was the Players' eighteenth successive win over the Gentlemen.

Despite his late start to the season Jackson appeared in six Nottinghamshire matches. He played against Yorkshire and Surrey in home and away fixtures, against Cambridgeshire at Lord's and against Kent at the Crystal Palace, Sydenham. The first match against Yorkshire was at Trent Bridge starting on 30 June with Yorkshire winning by 99 runs. Jackson took four for 72 in 56 overs in the match. If William Caffyn was the only man to claim a first-class hundred against a bowling side including John Jackson, then George Anderson of Yorkshire nearly became the second as he was left on 99 not out at the end of Yorkshire's second innings. By coincidence this was the final margin of Yorkshire's victory. Yorkshire made 125 and 236, and Nottinghamshire 124 and 138. In scoring 35 and 34, the highest score in both innings for Nottinghamshire, George Parr suffered injuries to his hand, so bad that he was unable to play again in 1864.

The return match took place at Bradford on 4, 5 and 6 August, and Nottinghamshire won by seven wickets. This time Yorkshire's Anderson was hit on the hand by Jackson after scoring 5 in his second innings; he had to retire hurt although he did return for Nottinghamshire's second innings and took a catch. Yorkshire's G.Atkinson was also injured after getting in the way of a hard drive from Richard Daft. He retired hurt and was unable to bat in the second innings, so the Midland County only needed to take eight wickets. Jackson bowled 54 overs in the match, taking three for 74, but his most important contribution was to score 52 in Nottinghamshire's first innings when he helped Daft, who made 80, secure a handy first innings lead. Yorkshire scored 183 and 112; Nottinghamshire 263 and 33 for three.

The first match against Surrey was played at Kennington Oval on 4 5, 6 July and saw two of the Surrey batsmen, H.H.Stephenson with 119 and

Mahala Jackson.

T.Lockyer 108* hit centuries, T.Humphrey adding 75 as Surrey ran up an enormous score for those days of 468. Jackson toiled manfully for 62 overs to take three for 98. Nottinghamshire replied with 283 with Alfred Shaw hitting 64, Richard Daft 56 and T.Bignall 49. In the follow-on C.Brampton scored 82 but Nottinghamshire could only muster 188 and Surrey were left with 4 runs to make to win by ten wickets. In the return at Trent Bridge on 28 and 29 July it was much closer before Surrey finally prevailed by one wicket. Jackson took four for 28 in 30 overs in the match and with Jem Grundy he made a determined effort to turn the tide when Surrey were set just 62 to win. The game was extended by 22 minutes after the official 7.00 pm finishing time to enable a result to be achieved in two days. In a low-scoring match Nottinghamshire made 107 and 81, Surrey 127 and 63 for 9.

The first great County match ever played on the Crystal Palace ground at Sydenham on 21, 22 and 23 July saw Nottinghamshire beat Kent by 74 runs scoring 143 and 165 with Kent making 124 and 110. Jackson took two for 46 in 49 overs, still economical even if his strike rate was not what it once was. The match against Cambridgeshire at Lord's on 18, 19 July was arranged to replace the North v South fixture which should have been played on those dates. Cambridgeshire won by 18 runs with Jackson only bowling in the first innings when he took one for 19 in 17 overs. His All-England sparring partner, George Tarrant took seven for 30 in the Nottinghamshire first innings. Two other colleagues from the England team, T.Hayward and R.Carpenter with 40 and 29 respectively, contributed the most to the second innings Cambridge score of 113. Nottinghamshire's totals were 59 and 158.

On 11, 12 July an England XI played XIII of Kent at Lord's winning by 219 runs. Tarrant took 12 Kent wickets. Jackson did not bowl but coming in late in the England second innings he clubbed his way to 68* to give his side a substantial lead., At Old Trafford on 11, 12 and 13 August North beat South, a team which included eight Surrey players. The South made 158 and 154 and the North 296 and 17 for one. Jackson took five for 26 off 25 overs in the match. Jackson's final first-class match of the season was at The Severalls (Mr Richard Cotton's ground), Newmarket on 6, 7 and 8 October where a Combined Kent and Nottinghamshire team played a Combined Cambridgeshire and Yorkshire team. The latter won easily scoring 145 and dismissing the Kent/Notts side for 84 and 57. Jackson bowled six overs taking 0 for 14.

In all first-class matches in 1864 Jackson had bowled 299 overs, 126 maidens and taken 22 wickets for 377 runs. He was not as dominant as in previous years and it seemed as if the burden of work he had undertaken in previous seasons as well as the recent Australian tour may have its toll on him.

His first appearance for the AEE came at the Trinity Ground in Halifax on 7th July against XXII of Halifax and District. Parr, injured in the Nottinghamshire v Yorkshire match, was missing as were other stalwarts like Tarrant, Hayward and Carpenter. The Halifax catchment area included two players from Huddersfield, five from Bradford, two from Todmorden and one each from Sheffield and London. The District appellation was still fairly flexible.

It was a grand scene at the Trinity ground with refreshment booths, flags and banners and the presence of the 4th West York Rifle Volunteers to entertain the large crowd. An itinerant hawker was selling 'All-England humbugs' at 1d a packet. The Halifax paper described Jackson as bowling with 'his terrible destructive swifts that appear to fly as if shot out of a mortar'. He took three wickets in the match and held three catches.

A week later - the AEE played XXII of Ashton-under-Lyne and were well beaten by 139 runs. Jackson took five for 54 in the match. The AEE batting collapsed twice with only Joseph Rowbotham with 48 in the first innings and George Tarrant with 38 in the second innings showing much resistance. The last six batsmen in the first innings all failed to score.

Jackson's next game for the AEE was at Harrogate on 1, 2 and 3 August where he top-scored in both innings with 46 and 38 by means of lusty hitting. He took only two wickets as the Harrogate XXII inflicted a third consecutive defeat on the AEE, winning by six wickets. They won their next match on 15 and 16 August though, beating the Sheffield Shrewsbury Club at Bramall Lane by an innings and 19 runs. Apart from three catches, Jackson contributed nothing.

On 18, 19 and 20 August the AEE travelled to the beautiful town of

Cirencester in Gloucestershire where the ground was in fine condition after a recent heatwave. The band of the West Gloucester Militia was present on this occasion. The AEE was handicapped in that Willsher was unable to bowl but Jackson took seven for 20 in 29 overs in the Cirencester first innings. *The Wiltshire and Gloucestershire Chronicle* graphically described one dismissal saying, 'One of the locals named Morris had the symmetry of his stumps destroyed'. The XII won the match by 80 runs with their two given professionals, Hodgson and Lillywhite, taking all 20 AEE wickets. This led to a protest from a Chronicle reader about the system of playing XXII against XI and making the point that it was difficult for the AEE batsmen to make runs against twenty fielders.

The AEE returned to Yorkshire where they played XXII of Dewsbury on 22August, beating them by six wickets. Tarrant and Tinley dismissed the locals between them. Jackson scored 20 and took two catches as his contribution to the victory. The next match was at Pudsey. Haygarth was highly critical of the ground, 'Out of the many bad cricket grounds the England Elevens have visited this was the worst it was ever their lot to perform on.' – quite a statement! Jackson took two wickets but the fact that 31 byes were conceded tells its own story of the state of the pitch. In the AEE first innings of 37, byes was top scorer with 12.

1 September saw the AEE playing at Kinning Park in Glasgow against XXII of the Clydesdale Club. The scores were level on first innings but the XXII made 95 in their second and reduced the AEE to 60 for 9 when time was called. Jackson took 11 wickets in the match. Back to Yorkshire – 5, 6 and 7 September - they came to Castle Hill in Scarborough where they beat the local XXII by 16 runs. The field was 'en fete' for what was turning into an annual occasion. Jackson had match figures of seven for 44 in 58 overs. At times the wind was so strong that the use of bails had to be dispensed with.

On 8, 9 and 10 September the AEE met XXII of Whalley and lost by 12 wickets. A good attendance was ensured with special trains laid on by the Lancashire and Yorkshire Railway. The AEE made 62 before Jackson (six for 24) and Tinley (14 for 45) demolished Whalley for 73. In their second innings the AEE made 69 and set the locals 64 to win. With excitement mounting more trains brought in yet more spectators and the band of the Clitheroe Rifle Volunteers played tunes to keep the crowd amused. Jackson bowled with his old fire to take seven for 20 in 22.3 overs but it was not enough. No sooner had the match ended than a storm broke out clearing the thousands of spectators quickly from the field to seek refuge in the pavilion, under the railway arches and still more at the railway station where the carriages of the special trains were soon filled. Altogether the takings were £140 for admission and the Club made an overall profit of between £10 and £20.

The AEE's northern travels next took them to Kendal in Westmoreland on 12, 13 and 14 September where only ten hours play was possible over the three days scheduled for the match. There was no play until 4.00 pm on the second day as the third day's play did not start until 3.00 pm. In the circumstances a finish could not be obtained and the large crowd had a frustrating wait. So boisterous was the weather on the third day that part of the Kendal Club pavilion was blown down. The AEE made 58, Kendal relying with 103. In their second innings the AEE were 9 for 3 in the time that play that was possible.

Jackson played in 12 AEE matches, playing 21 innings with 5 not outs and scoring 149 runs at an average of 9.31. He took 51 wickets which was his lowest return for some time and he took 15 catches. It seemed as if his powers were on the wane, but the 1865 season was to prove such thoughts premature.

John Jackson only appeared in ten first-class matches, 29 wickets for 340 runs at 11.72 and 276.1 overs of which 124 were maidens and took 26 wickets at an average of 11.50. Seven of these were County fixtures for Nottinghamshire, six of which were won.

Jackson was wicketless in the first fixture of the year when Sussex were thrashed at Trent Bridge on 1, 2 and 3 June in the first match between the two counties since 1853. Batting first, Nottinghamshire scored 208 with Daft making 67and Parr, by now in his 21st season with the County scoring 54. Sussex collapsed twice for 84 and 38 with Jackson's bowling not being needed as Jem Grundy took five for 6 in 25 overs in the second Sussex innings, having taken five for 37 in 33 overs in the first. The Nottinghamshire margin of victory was an innings and 86 runs.

Surrey, who came to Trent Bridge on 26, 27 and 28 June, proved to be a sterner test and Nottinghamshire owed much to W.Oscroft who batted through their first innings for 53* out of a total of 94. Jackson did not bowl in Surrey's first innings of 137 but returned like a giant refreshed to take seven for 25 in 20.3 overs in their second innings of 81. Six of his victims were bowled and one was lbw. Nottinghamshire made light of the 125 they needed to win, losing only two wickets. Continuing the good form Nottinghamshire beat Yorkshire at Bradford in two days - 6 and 7 July - by an innings and 30 runs. Daft made 66 of the Nottinghamshire total of 233. Yorkshire could only manage 130 and 73. Jackson took four for 30 in 17.1 overs in the match.

The return match with Surrey at the Oval on 13, 14 and 15 July saw Nottinghamshire lose by one wicket in an interesting match. Oscroft hit up 69 and Jackson 22 as Nottinghamshire made 157 in the first innings, a score that Surrey bettered by 13. The Nottinghamshire second innings score was 207 helped by an 86 from C.Brampton and 28 from Jackson. Surrey needed 195 to win and with Jem Grundy taking eight for 68 had been reduced to 181 for 9 when T.Sewell came in to join Heathfield Stephenson who was 75*. Sewell hit off the remaining runs amidst some controversy as the Nottinghamshire players were convinced that Sewell had been clearly stumped but the umpiring decision went against them. The dispute was so serious that fixtures were not renewed for 1866.

Nottinghamshire returned to winning ways by completing the double over Yorkshire in a topsy-turvy match at Trent Bridge on 27, 28 and 29 July which they won by 55 runs. Nottinghamshire collapsed to 117 all out. Yorkshire made 191, a lead of 74. Parr made 48 and Jackson 55 in the Nottinghamshire second innings of 182. Yorkshire needed only 109 to win but J.C.Shaw was deadly in their second innings, taking eight for 32 in 33.3 overs to win the match for Nottinghamshire. Jackson took just one for 35 in Yorkshire's first innings, his main contribution to the victory having come with the bat.

Nottinghamshire's next fixture was against Cambridgeshire on 17, 18 and 19 August and, oddly enough it took place at neutral Old Trafford, the match having been arranged by the Manchester Club. Oscroft (78) and Brampton (79) added 146 for Nottinghamshire's first wicket in their 236 all out. Jackson took two for 15 in 13 overs in the Cambridgeshire first innings and six for 38 in the second as they collapsed for totals of 86 and 64 giving Nottinghamshire victory by an innings and 86 runs.

A goodly attendance at the Royal Brunswick Ground, Hove on 24 and 25 August saw Nottinghamshire complete the double over Sussex in winning by an innings and 86 runs. Sussex scored 118 and 77 with Jackson taking one for 29 in 43.1 overs. Nottinghamshire made 245 with Oscroft hitting a fine century, finishing with 107 whilst Jackson hit the second highest score of 27 featuring some fine hitting.

Jackson appeared for the AEE against the UAEE at Lord's on 5, 6 and 7 June. The match was graced by the presence of the Prince of Wales on the second day. There were gate receipts of £133. 2s on the first day, £88 on the second day and £47 9s 6d on the third day and a substantial donation was made to the Cricketers Fund Friendly Society. With a number of players from the UAEE having seceded to the newly formed United South of England Eleven the UAEE had no players from Surrey, Kent or Sussex available and were beaten easily by 66 runs. The AEE made 207 and 186 while the UAEE made 176 and 151. Jackson took four for 59 in the match in 41 overs.

Jackson's other first-class match in 1865 was for the North against the South at Canterbury on 7, 8 and 9 August, a match which the South won by 27 runs. Jackson did little, scoring 7 and 3 and only bowling eight overs.

Jackson played in 25 AEE matches against odds in 1865 with the team winning 15, losing five and drawing five matches. He scored 373 runs and took 210 wickets and held 25 catches in a welcome return to form after his 1864 performances.

The saga started on 11 May in Jackson's home town of Retford and he was to play cricket almost without a break until 27 September, a period of 108 days with all the travelling that this involved. It would be interesting to hear Jackson's views on the hard-done to players of today whose fixture schedules are nowhere near as hectic.

Getting back to the cricket, the match at Retford was drawn very much in favour of the local XXII as the AEE were 31 for seven when stumps were drawn for good having been set 137 to win. Jackson bowled 33.2

overs in the match taking seven for 45. Haygarth noted that the AEE was now composed entirely of northern cricketers as southern professional cricketers such as Julius Caesar, H.H.Stephenson and E Willsher had left them for the United South of England Eleven. There was a further cricketing problem involving a division of loyalties between players' county teams and the itinerant professional elevens who paid more for their services than their counties did.

The next AEE match was at Huddersfield on 15, 16 and 17 May against a local XX which defeated the Eleven by the narrowest possible margin of one run. Jackson did his best, taking 17 wickets in the match but Luke Greenwood took five in both innings for Huddersfield including Jackson, bowled for 13 in the final innings. The Eleven then had a long journey to face in order to get to Partick in Glasgow where they were due to face XX of West of Scotland 18, 19 and 20 May. Luke Greenwood came with them to guest for the Scottish team and he took four wickets in both of the AEE innings in a drawn match which was played on the Hamilton Crescent Ground. The AEE scored 137 and 204, West of Scotland made 82 and 52 -9. Jackson took three wicket.

At Southampton on 29 May the AEE were beaten by XXII of the Southampton Union Club by five wickets. Jackson bowled a long spell in this match - 69 overs to take eight for 65. An even match saw all four totals fall within the range of 125 to 155. Jackson's next AEE match was at Whalley on 8 June where trains bought many spectators from Preston, Burnley, Blackburn, Accrington and Clitheroe to watch the match and be entertained by the bands of the Burnley Rifle Volunteers and the 3rd King's Own Hussars. The XXII collapsed before Tinley's lob bowling as he took 29 wickets in the match. Whalley made only 33 in their first innings and, although they did better with 143 in their second knock with John Smith of Yeadon scoring 48, the highest individual score in the match, the AEE still won by 63 runs. Jackson took one wicket in the second innings.

12 June saw the AEE begin a match against XXII of Ossett who beat them by 11 wickets. Jackson took 14 wickets in the match, but Luke Greenwood, making something of a habit of this, took five cheap AEE wickets in the second innings and Ossett needed only 69 to win. The end of the match was followed by a contest between three of the England players, Jackson, Oscroft and Iddison and nine of the Ossett players. The three England players were bowled out for 7 and Ossett made 8 for 8 to win by one wicket.

The AEE now had two relatively easy victories in Yorkshire, beating XXII of Boston Spa by 62 runs on 15, 16 and 17 June and XXII of Mirfield by 95 runs on 19, 20 and 21 June. In this latter match the *Huddersfield Chronicle* described Jackson's bowling as being 'more destructive even than usual'. He took 21 wickets and shared a good stand with George Tarrant in the AEE second innings making 33 whilst Tarrant hit up 53.

The next match, against XVIII of Manchester Broughton featured some unusually high scoring. The AEE made 278 and the Club replied with 233,

Jackson taking eight wickets. Jackson contributed 55 to the AEE second inning of 273 who thus led by 318 when the match was called off after their second innings finished.

A local XXII at Rochdale was beaten by an innings and 63 runs on 29 June but one of their players, John Leach, had the distinction of scoring 57, the highest individual score of the match. He was given a warm reception from the large crowd and a rendering of '*See the Conquering Hero Comes'* from the band. He was presented with a new bat by the Club President. Jackson bowled 37 overs to take five for 26. In a close match at the Swallowfield Park near Reading on 3, 4 and 5 July, the AEE beat a local XXI by three runs with Jackson taking 15 wickets, Tinley and Tarrant 11 apiece. No team total higher than 87 was made and the highest individual score was 24. In the circumstances Jackson's unbeaten 23 was a fine effort.

On 17 July at Bramall Lane, Sheffield the AEE took the field against Yorkshire in an eleven-a-side match which they won by an innings and 265 runs. All their batsmen made double figures and their stars from Cambridgeshire, T.Hayward and R.Carpenter, hit 112 and 134 respectively. Several of the leading Yorkshire players were not selected as they had refused to play for Yorkshire against Surrey. England made 524 and in Yorkshire's innings of 125 and 144, Wootton took all ten wickets in the second innings. Jackson had three for 41 in 27 overs.

On 20 July the AEE played XXII of Burton-on-Trent in a benefit game for William Peace, a player of some note in the Burton area. The AEE won by 37 runs with Jackson bagging 13 victims and Tinley with 21 again proving the effectiveness of his lobs against inexperienced batsmen. Peace's scores were 0 and 0* - no 'one off the mark' for the beneficiary in this match.

The next match at Thornhill Lees, Saville Town, Dewsbury on 24, 25 and 26 July was much closer. The local XXII won by one wicket after dismissing the AEE for 113 and 147, Dewsbury scored 183 and 73 for 20 with Jackson taking 12 wickets. The AEE had a strong bowling array in this match with Tarrant, Hayward and Tinley amongst the wickets as well.

Jackson's next AEE appearance was on 31 July, 1 and 2 August at Bishop's Stortford in Hertfordshire where the Eleven were soundly beaten by the local XXII with 20 wickets in hand. Jackson took three wickets in the match. Back in North Yorkshire the AEE met XXII of Thirsk on 3 August and won again, this time by six wickets. Tinley took 21 wickets and Tarrant 19 in the Thirsk innings of 97 and 76. Jackson did not bowl and he did not bowl at Aston-under-Lyne in the next match either as the last two days were washed out by rain. In the play that was possible on 10 August the XXII scored 44 being demolished by Tinley and Tarrant. The AEE made 259 in reply.

The AEE played XXII of Earlsheaton at Chickenley near Dewsbury on 21 August. Jackson took 21 wickets in the match, bowling the AEE to victory by a margin of 59 runs. On 28, 29 and 30 August at the Castle Hill Ground, Scarborough the AEE drew with a local XXII dismissing them for 38 in their first innings with 17 batsmen failing to pass 2. So much play was lost to rain on the first day that, despite good weather on the second and third days, the game could not be finished. In contrast with the previous AEE match Jackson took but one wicket.

His fortunes changed in the next AEE match on 31 August which was against XXII of Bootle. This ended in a 47 run victory, Jackson having taken nine wickets in the first Bootle innings. The next match took the team to Carlisle where the local XXII was defeated by 8 wickets on 4, 5 and 6 August. Jackson was amongst the wickets again, this time dismissing 13 batsmen. This match was followed by a single-wicket match between four of the AEE team and Ten of Carlisle which ended in a tie. Jackson scored four of the AEE total of 9 and took two wickets.

Moving on to Harrogate on 7 September the AEE beat XXII of Harrogate. Jackson took 12 wickets in the match. He did not bowl in his next AEE appearance on 18, 19 and 20 September against XXII of Bishop Auckland, but in scoring 22 did make the second-highest individual score for the AEE and the team won by an innings and one run with Tarrant doing the hat trick. At Peterborough on 21 September Jackson made 25 and took eight wickets as the locals were defeated by 18 runs.

The AEE's last match ended in a defeat by XVIII Gentlemen of the North at the Hyde Park Ground at Sheffield by 30 runs. Jackson took eight wickets. The Gentlemen of the North scored 129 and it then took the AEE openers 32 balls to score the first run and the team was dismissed for 51. Eventually the AEE were set 141 to win. Whilst Hayward with 46 and Carpenter (20) were together they had a very good chance but after these two were separated a collapse followed and the final score was only 110.

On Easter Monday Jackson played in the annual Colts match at Trent Bridge, bowling 27 overs and taking three for 27 in a drawn match. On 14 August he played for Nottinghamshire against XIV Free Foresters at Trent Bridge. Only eleven of the Free Foresters batted in their first innings and twelve in the second innings, but all fourteen fielded and they won by 56 runs with Jackson failing to take a wicket. Finally he played as a 'given' man for XXII of Leeds against the United All-England Eleven at the Holbeck Recreation Ground, Leeds on 11, 12 and 13 September. He bowled John Thewlis and Alfred Shaw, scored 4 and 18 and took a catch.

Chapter Ten
Injury Strikes

Years of overbowling finally began to take their toll of John Jackson, and whilst playing for Nottinghamshire against Yorkshire at Trent Bridge, he fell heavily when chasing the ball. He was in great pain having burst a blood vessel behind his knee, an injury which not only ended his season but also virtually spelt the end of his first-class career. Although he was to appear in one final AEE v UAEE match in 1867 and continued to appear in odds-matches for the AEE in 1867 and, more spasmodically, until 1871, his career was now entering its final stages.

John Jackson's first-class season started at Lord's on 21, 22 and 23 May in the annual AEE v UAEE match which was played for the benefit of the Cricketers Fund Friendly Society. The match was well attended with 10,620 spectators passing through the turnstiles over the three days play. Gate takings were £150.1s on the first day (Whit Monday), £100.8s on the second day and £17 on the third - a total of £267.9s. This was the sixteenth match between the two great professional elevens, both teams having won seven matches with two games finishing in draws. Both sides in this game were composed of Northern players as the Southern professionals had formed themselves into a new team - the United South of England Eleven.

In this match, which the UAEE won by 69 runs, Jackson bowled 20 overs in the second innings, taking one for 19, his wicket being that of his old antagonist, Robert Carpenter, who was caught and bowled. John Smith scored 62 for the UAEE whose totals of 186 and 148 outscored the AEE's 115 and 153. The AEE's highest scorer, W.Oscroft, hit 86 in a valiant attempt to rescue a lost cause. New stars were appearing on both sides J.C.Shaw of Nottinghamshire took five wickets in his first appearance in a big match while making his debut for the UAEE was George Freeman, from Boroughbridge in Yorkshire, a fine bowler who was to prove a worthy successor to Jackson and Tarrant in the years to come. In this particular game though, the star bowler for the UAEE was George Howitt who took thirteen for 129 with some hideously fast break-backs and bumpers. He felled Richard Daft with a blow on the chin with a particularly nasty delivery.

John Jackson played in three County matches for Nottinghamshire. In the first of these at Fenner's on 31 May, 1 and 2 June, Nottinghamshire beat Cambridgeshire by eight wickets, with Jackson taking seven wickets for 36 runs in 30.1 overs in the match. Nottinghamshire made 270 and 34 for two. Cambridgeshire were bowled out for 138 and 164. In the return fixture at Trent Bridge on 5 July, Cambridgeshire did much better. Hayward made 73 and Carpenter 57 out of a total of217, and Nottinghamshire replied with 195. With Warren making 72 in their second innings of 179, Cambridgeshire set Nottinghamshire 202 to win. They ended the match on 99 for six with W.Oscroft 55*. Jackson had a rare wicketless match, bowling 31 overs for 75 runs.

On 2 and 3 August Yorkshire were the visitors at Trent Bridge and were defeated by nine wickets, despite Jackson's serious injury which allowed him to bowl only 4 overs in the match for 7 runs. J.C.Shaw with six for 36 in Yorkshire's first innings of 78, and G.Wootton with five for 47 in their second innings of 83, stepped into the breach for Nottinghamshire and won the match.

Jackson played in 15 matches for the AEE, batting 25 times with 5 not out innings and scoring 202 runs at an average of 10.10. He took 57 wickets and held 19 catches.

The first game was at the Trinity College ground at Cambridge on 14, 15 and 16 May where an XVIII of Trinity College beat the AEE by fourteen wickets. Jackson took one for 30 in 36 overs. The College owed much to the Lyttleton brothers. Hon.C.G.Lyttleton made 90 and Hon.G.S.Lyttleton made 55 to thwart a fine AEE attack of J.C.Shaw, Tinley, Freeman and Jackson. Richard Daft scored 55 and 41* for the AEE but had little support.

Moving on to Oxford the Eleven beat XIV Graduates of the University by three wickets on 17, 18 and 19 May. Haygarth noted some slow scoring in this game with AEE taking five hours to score their first innings of 246. He pointed out that Oxford took only three hours to make 245 in their second innings, but they did have three more fielders. Jackson bowled seven overs for 9 runs but had a good double with the bat, scoring 24* and 11*.

On 24 May the AEE played a match against XXII of West of Scotland at the Hamilton Crescent Ground in Glasgow. West of Scotland won by 13 wickets with Luke Greenwood acting as a given man. Jackson took five wickets in what was a low-scoring match. With the game ending early a single-wicket match took place between Smith, Oscroft and Jackson of the AEE and eight West of Scotland players. The West made 42 with Jackson taking four wickets and Smith had made 14 for the AEE when play was abandoned.

The next match was at Ossett on 28 May where Greenwood again acted as a given man and took nine for 116 in the AEE innings of 110 and 146. Ossett made 192 but needing only 65 to win collapsed to 38 all out. Tinley took 12 for 25 and Jackson seven for 4 in 18 overs. E.Stephenson stumped ten batsmen, nine of them off Tinley. The AEE won by 27 runs.

At Hyde Park in Sheffield on 4 and 5 June the AEE proved much too strong for XVIII Colts of Nottingham and Sheffield, beating them by an innings and 8 runs. The Colts were captained by W.G.Grace from Gloucestershire who made 36 in their second innings of 91. Jackson took four wickets in the match, J.C.Shaw took fourteen and G.Atkinson thirteen. Jackson did not bowl in the next match at Heckmondwike.

He next appeared for the team at the Northern Ground in Liverpool on

25, 26 and 27 June where the AEE met XXII of Seaforth and lost in a close finish by 4 runs. Haygarth's comment that 'the ground broke up fearfully and the bowlers had it all their own way' seems fully justified given the low scores. Seaforth made 85 and 68, and the AEE scores were 109 and 40. Only seven double figure scores were recorded. There were 17 zeros in Seaforth's second innings and three other men were written down as 'absent'. Jackson took five first innings wickets.

On 28 June Jackson was back where it had all begun, when the AEE met XVIII of Newark at the Kelham Road Ground and won by ten wickets, with Carpenter batting for five hours and twenty minutes to score 34*, a fine example of how difficult it was for even the best batsmen to score swiftly against multiple fielders. Jackson took ten wickets in the match, and Tarrant, J.C.Shaw and Tinley shared the others. Newark made 96 in both innings, the AEE making 168 and 28 for nought.

Jackson remained in his home area for his next AEE match which was against XXII of Retford on 9, 10 and 11 July. They beat the AEE by ten wickets with their two given men, Luke Greenwood, again, and G.Howitt, who took seventeen wickets between them. Greenwood must have loved playing against the AEE by this time! For his part John Jackson bowled the first three Retford batsmen for 0, 10 and 0 respectively.

The next AEE game was at Oldham on 12, 13 and 14 July where Jackson took a wicket with his second ball against the local XXII and went on to take another five as Oldham collapsed to 50 all out. AEE made 171 with John Smith scoring 56, Tom Hayward 47 and George Anderson 32. Oldham were then dismissed for 119 to give the AEE victory by an innings and 2 runs. Jackson took one wicket. The bands of the Lancashire Rifle Volunteers and the Blue Coat Boys were on hand to cheer the local spectators with their lively music.

The AEE were at Dudley on 16 July where a XXII of Dudley defeated them by seven wickets. Jackson took only one wicket, but Tinley created havoc with his lobs, taking nineteen wickets. On the last day of the game one of the local players, J.S.Wainwright, backed himself to throw the cricket ball 110 yards. He did it too, throwing the ball 112 yards at his third attempt.

Moving to the North West on 23 and 24 July, the AEE played their first match at Whitehaven, Cumberland since 1856. Jackson, Parr and Greenwood had all played for the AEE on that occasion and then, as now, the AEE won the match, this time by 144 runs. Jackson made an unbeaten 26, besides taking 11 Whitehaven wickets in the first innings. At the conclusion of the game a single-wicket match took place between three AEE players - Oscroft, Smith and Jackson - and eleven of Whitehaven. Jackson took seven wickets - all bowled as Whitehaven were dismissed for 13. The AEE scored 16 (Jackson 3).

Over in the North East XXII of Darlington were beaten on 26, 27 and 28 July by an innings and 20 runs. Jackson was wicketless but perhaps he did not bowl after his efforts at Whitehaven. Although defeated they were happy to have made a handsome profit from the match to put towards making a new ground as their present ground had been earmarked for building purposes.

A long journey followed down to Bishop's Stortford in Hertfordshire for an incident packed match on 30, 31 July and 1 August which ended with the scores tied at 261 apiece. One incident occurred when C.Marshall of the AEE was bowled by Alfred Shaw who was guesting for the local XVIII. Marshall claimed not to have been ready and appealed to Umpire Rowbotham who gave him not out. On a second appeal being made by the bowler the umpire ruled it out and Marshall had to go. Another dispute arose when G.Anderson hit a ball to the boundary and the batsmen ran two which the scorers marked down having no authority from the umpires to mark down more although Anderson thought that he should have got four. When the match ended with the AEE bowled out for 132 or two runs short of a tied match, the Bishop's Stortford captain, Mr W.F.Maitland was appealed to for the two runs and good-naturedly allowed the appeal so the match finished all-square. Amidst all these goings-on Jackson took two second innings wickets.

Apart from his appearance for Nottinghamshire against Yorkshire at Trent Bridge on 2 and 3 August where he bowled four overs in the Yorkshire second innings that was the end of Jackson's cricket in 1866. Injury together with the endless travelling up and down the country from May to September had taken its toll.

Chapter Eleven

Last Full Season

Recovered from injury Jackson played in 22 matches for the AEE against odds in 1867. He batted 33 times with 8 not out innings and scored 187 runs at an average of 7.48. He took 80 wickets and 27 catches.

The matches began at the Trinity College ground at Cambridge on 6 May where the AEE played a game against XVI of Trinity College and won by five wickets. John Smith scored 83 and Carpenter 53 in the AEE total of 220. The College were bowled out for 99 with Tarrant taking nine wickets and J.C.Shaw taking five. The College recovered to make 284 in their second innings with W.S.O.Warner hitting 108, a rare hundred against an AEE attack. Jackson took one for 23 in 28 overs. Set to score 164 to win the AEE were in trouble with five batsmen dismissed cheaply before Carpenter with 55* and Parr 30* steered them home. There were 77 extras in the match, 59 of them in the AEE innings including 42 byes. Long-stop must have been kept busy!

The AEE paid a rare visit to Ireland for a match at Belfast on 13 May against XXII of Northern Ireland supported by Luke Greenwood and Roger Iddison. In a low-scoring game the Irish team won by eight wickets although twelve of their batsmen including the last seven in the order registered ducks.

On 23 May the AEE began a match against the UAEE at Old Trafford for the benefit of the Cricketers' Fund which ended in an AEE victory and which turned out to be Jackson's final first-class match. He had match figures of seven for 95. Six of these came at a cost of 50 runs in the second innings when he and Alfred Shaw bowled unchanged for 57.1 overs. Haygarth commented that all the players were from the North and went on to say that Lord's and the Oval were 'now deserted by the Northern Men. It 'paid' more to confine their efforts to the North.'

The next AEE match in which Jackson appeared, but took no wickets, was played against XXII of Heckmondwicke who beat the Eleven by 33 runs. Luke Greenwood, once again a given man player, took 13 wickets. Carpenter hit 61 for the AEE with Jackson unbeaten on 33. After leading by 44 runs on the first innings the AEE needed only 83 to win but were bowled out for 50 with only E.Stephenson reaching double figures.

On 30 May the AEE played XXII of Bootle winning by 224 runs. The Bootle batting folded completely for 39 and 45 with their second innings lasting only 105 minutes. Luke Greenwood, for once turning out for the AEE, took 20 wickets and Carpenter scored 73. The Bootle batsmen made 17 ducks and only one man reached double figures. Once again Jackson didn't bowl. The next match should have started at Knaresborough on 3 June but bad weather delayed the start by 24 hours and, as a consequence, the game finished in a draw. The AEE made 133 and 99 for 8. Knaresborough made 68 with J.C.Shaw capturing 11 wickets. Jackson made 0 and was wicketless.

At Accrington on 13 June the band of the Rifle Volunteers provided entertainment for the crowd during breaks in play which were frequent, the weather being at times, wet and threatening. Once again the match ended in a draw with J.C.Shaw taking 23 wickets and T. Hayward scoring 82 and E.Stephenson 53 for the AEE. An unusual dismissal was recorded by Haygarth for W.Lord who is shown as 'handled the ball' in *Scores and Biographies Vol.X.* The local paper says he was out lbw. Once again Jackson was wicketless.

Venturing south for once the AEE next played at the Aston Ground in Birmingham where they met a Birmingham XXII who were beaten by an innings and 35 runs. Birmingham were bowled out for 59 and 65 with J.C.Shaw taking another 23 wickets and 16 Birmingham players making ducks. Again Jackson does not appear to have bowled. Only two players reached double figures. John Smith hit up 67 in the second AEE innings. With Shaw in such devastating form Jackson's bowling was hardly needed but he did return to the bowling crease against XXII of Staveley on 24 June. The match was played on 130 yards of turf laid out at the expense of the local iron works for the recreation of of the numerous workmen there. The AEE won by 141 runs with Richard Daft scoring 49 and 34 and Carpenter making 46 in the second innings. Shaw took 14 wickets and Jackson took eight, seven of them bowled. At Halifax on 27 and 28 June the AEE beat a local XXII by ten wickets. Jackson had four wickets while Tinley and Shaw dismissed 27 batsmen. Tinley had a fine match making 40 with the consistent Carpenter adding 47* to his series of valuable innings for the AEE.

1, 2 and 3 July saw the AEE beat XXII of Enderby Park at Enderby Hall near Leicester by 47 runs in a low-scoring match. Jackson scored 2 and 0 and took no wickets. They continued their good form with a ten wickets win over XVIII of the Manchester Broughton Club on 4, 5 and 6 July, with Jackson taking seven wickets in the match and Oscroft (23) and Stephenson (59) adding 82 for the first AEE wicket. In the Manchester first innings four batsmen are listed as 'absent' which helps to account for their dismissal for 34 all out with their top scorer making 8. In their second innings W.Hickton defied the bowling of Shaw, who took ten wickets, Tinley and Jackson to make 46 out of 153 all out.

In the match against XXII of Hull on 8 and 9 July Jackson was back to something like his best, taking eleven second innings wickets as the AEE won by an innings and 41 runs. Eight of his victims were bowled. Tarrant had done the damage in Hull's first innings with ten wickets, their totals being 51 and 58. The fielding of the AEE was greatly admired by the large crowd.

At Oldham on 11 July Jackson took twenty-two wickets in the match against an Oldham XXII. The considerable crowd of spectators were entertained by the Waterhead Amateur Brass Band and the marching of the Blue Coat Schoolboys as well as some lively hitting in an innings of 53 by John Smith of the AEE who sent one ball flying over the pavilion, along with some other mighty blows.

Having won seven matches in a row with Jackson in the team, the AEE now moved south to the Spa Ground in Gloucester on 15, 16 and 17 July where they lost to the local XXII which containing the 16 year-old G.F.Grace, by nine wickets. The bowling of Shaw and Jackson was much admired, with Jackson taking twelve wickets in the match, but the AEE collapsed to 37 all out in their second innings. Three run outs did not help their cause, including that of John Thewlis for 4, top scorer in the first innings. Rain frequently held up proceedings on the first day and the band of the Artillery Company was on duty from 2.00 pm to 7.00 pm each day. A stand was erected for spectators who chose to pay 6d extra. This was a picturesque ground with horse chestnut, lime and elm trees making a fine backdrop to the cricket. A statue of Queen Anne had her back to the actual play. She clearly did not know what she was missing.

In the next match at Bolton on 18 July, although Jackson took three wickets, the AEE lost by twenty wickets to a Bolton & District XXII before crowds so large that the professionals admitted they had not performed in front of larger crowds at a cricket match anywhere other than in Australia. At least 10,000 spectators watched each day's play, including 2,500 ladies. Proceeds amounted to £350 with 4,500 spectators paying 6d each to watch the play. Special buses brought the crowds from the local railway station. Jackson took three wickets in the game which Bolton had won early on the third day, but to entertain the crowd they batted on until 5.00 pm by which time twenty of their wickets had fallen.

The AEE were beaten in their next match too, by XXII of Sutton-in-Ashfield on 22 July, a match played for the benefit of Thomas Heath who had played in the Nottingham Eleven as long ago as 1828. Richard Daft was dismissed by the first ball he received in both innings, an unusual lapse by such a fine batsman. The match excited huge interest with a crowd of 6,000 present on the second day. Jackson took three wickets and Tarrant, Tinley and Shaw shared the others.

The next match on 29 July saw the AEE visit Bishop's Stortford again where they gave an efficient display to beat a local XVIII by an innings and 26 runs. Shaw was their most effective bowler with eighteen wickets; Jackson took the wickets of just three tail-enders in the second innings. The locals were handicapped when their highest scorer, G.A.Vandermeulen, dislocated his shoulder when 26* in his first innings and could not bat a second time.

The AEE began August 1867 with a 44 run victory over XXII of Ashton-under-Lyne, with Tarrant taking nineteen wickets and Tinley taking fourteen. Jackson only took one wicket, but John Smith's batting really won the match as he made 57 against deliveries 'which kicked fearfully on the hard and dry ground'. Eighteen of the 44 Ashton-under-Lyne batsmen who went to the crease came back without troubling the scorer.

Smith gave another fine performance in the next match at Bramall Lane, Sheffield on 5 August, making 109, and, with Hayward (55) and Tarrant (42*), lifting the AEE to a score of 269 for seven, after the first innings scores had tied at 151 apiece. Jackson again didn't bowl. The match, against XXII of the Sheffield Shrewsbury Club, finished as a draw. A party from the local Charity School attended the match by invitation of the Club Committee.

Moving down to Nottinghamshire on 12 August, the AEE played XXII of Arnold on the home ground of the Duke of St Albans at Bestwood Park. The match was drawn with Smith, in a rich vein of form, being out for 99 and scoring 59 in his second innings too when the AEE, set 126 to win, finished on 92 for 6. This was the first match to be played on this newly formed ground and was a good even contest with Arnold scoring 126 and 221 and the AEE totalling 222 and 92 for 6. Tinley took 22 wickets for the AEE and George Pinder, keeping wicket stumped nine and caught one batsman. This was off Jackson who took three wickets.

Apart from an appearance against XXII of Scarborough on 19, 20 and 21 August this was the end of Jackson's cricket in 1867. Presumably fitness was becoming an increasing problem. Being dependent upon the game for his living he would obviously have played had it been possible.

Chapter Twelve

Final Matches

After the 1867 season Jackson seldom appears in Haygarth's recorded scores. For the 1868 season he accepted an appointment as professional at the Lancashire club of Burnley, appearing as pro for the Club against George Parr's All-England Eleven on 9, 10 and 11 July. He scored 17 and 10 for the Burnley XXII and took four wickets. These included both the AEE opening batsmen, John Smith and Joseph Rowbotham as well as George Tarrant and J.C.Shaw. Tarrant took Jackson's wicket in both the AEE innings of a game which the AEE won by ten wickets.

In other matches Jackson made a guest appearance for XXII of Heckmondwicke against the United South of England XI taking three good wickets in both innings of a drawn game. At Oldham on 26, 27 June he played for the newly formed North of England Eleven against XX of Werneth. The North of England won a close match by five runs so achieving a 100% record as the Eleven did not play again and was abandoned at the end of the season. Jackson's main contribution to the success was to dismiss four Werneth batsmen for nought in their second innings.

Jackson's only match for the AEE in 1868 was against XXII of Mansfield on 13, 14 and 15 July, a match that Mansfield won by 13 wickets. Haygarth paid a fitting tribute:

> John Jackson's name is now seldom found on the England side.... His bowling was very fine in his day and the speed tremendous.

He appeared regularly for Burnley that year making the top score - 31 - against Halifax as well as scoring 63 against Broughton and 56 plus seven wickets against Oldham. Against Halifax he took six for 13 and five for 13 and nine wickets in the match against Keighley. His innings against Broughton attracted this from the *Burnley Advertiser*:

> Jackson made 63 by truly fine cricket, hitting all-round and bidding defiance to the Broughton attack.

They just don't write reports like that, anymore!

Jackson was engaged by Burnley again in 1869 when he took six for 22 and five for 51 against Oldham in a spell which moved the *Burnley Advertiser* to write that 'Jackson has never appeared to better advantage with the ball.' Against Accrington he scored 27 and took five wickets. At Oldham he scored 31, 'running it up quickly.' In the Liverpool match he bowled four of his opponents in succession, taking five for 14. Keighley were hit about for 71 runs in a way that 'was beyond all praise.' At Blackburn he scored 40 and came up against the future Lancashire and England captain, A.N.Hornby who scored 20* for Blackburn. Hornby, it should be noted, gave Jackson some stick in the return match, scoring 74 while Jackson took three for 64. In the return match against Accrington he made 31 and took three wickets. He had more than earned his keep at Burnley.

For the 1870 season Jackson accepted a position as groundsman, coach, cook and player at the Dingle Cricket Club in Liverpool. This was an appointment that was to last for three years and necessitated a family move from Nottinghamshire to Merseyside. He made two appearances for the AEE. The first was against the Sheffield Shrewsbury Club at Bramall Lane when he took six wickets in the second innings. His final recorded appearance for the AEE was at Sleaford on 6, 7 and 8 July in 1871 where the local XXII beat the AEE by 12 wickets after the AEE had collapsed to 42 all out. Jackson took one wicket. His final recorded appearance was for An Eleven of England against East Lancashire at Accrington on 1, 2 and 3 September 1871 in another drawn match. He made 3 and 4, took a catch but failed to take a wicket.

At this stage Jackson the cricketer disappears from view, but in his interview with A.W.Pullin he filled in some of the gaps about what he was doing over the next five years. He was engaged by Lord Massareene in Ireland in 1864. In 1875 and 1876 he was at Richmond in North Yorkshire. He spent 1877 with Cambridge University and Norfolk County at Norwich. Then followed three years at Birkenhead Grammar School. In 1880, aged 47, he must have hung up his boots.

He had well earned a long and happy retirement. Sadly he did not get one! I should set the scene with a quotation from Pullin's interview. Always sensitive to the sad decline of old cricketers when their days of glory ceased Pullin says:

> Now let me give the reverse side of the picture. A bent and grisly man of sixty-seven, subsisting on a pittance of 5s.6d. a week, willing to work but elbowed out by younger and more vigorous competitors in the battle of life, having no permanent address and always hovering on the threshold of the workhouse.
> Jolly game, cricket.

Chapter Thirteen

Family Life and Decline 1880 to 1901

In 1870, as we have seen, Jackson accepted a position with the Dingle Cricket Club in Liverpool. Clearly he could not carry out these tasks while based in in Nottinghamshire so he finally moved from the county he had come to regard as home and set up home with his family on Merseyside where he was to spend the rest of his life.

Liverpool had developed over the previous half century into a prosperous and thriving port with a diverse population. It dominated the North American cargo and passenger traffic and the resultant prosperity attracted many Welsh and Irish settlers. The expanding dock area, which eventually stretched from Bootle in the north to Toxteth in the south, offered plenty of unskilled work. A sizeable Welsh presence had built up in the south of the city in the Toxteth area. In one of these streets of terraced houses, 8 Madryn Street, Mahala Jackson was to die.

The 1871 census shows the Jackson family living at No.26 Smith Lane, North Toxteth. John and Mahala now had a family consisting of, firstly, Elizabeth born in 1858 and shown as 13 year-old scholar. Second was John, born in Ollerton on 19 June 1861 and therefore nine years old and not 11 as claimed on the Census. He was also shown as a scholar. Kate, born in Ollerton on 12 September 1863, is listed as an eight year-old scholar. Harry, born in Retford on 29 March 1866, had just had his fifth birthday and was a scholar. Samuel who had been born in Liverpool in 1870 was just five months old. Also still living with them was Margaret Jackson, listed as a lodger, but in reality Jackson's mother. She is shown as being aged 82, a fine age for a Victorian matriarch, if the age is to be believed.

By 1881 the family had moved to 23 Carlton Hill, still in North Toxteth. John's mother had died and so, sadly, had Elizabeth, the eldest daughter. We have to remember that it was very rare for all the children in a family to survive to adulthood with killer diseases like tuberculosis, smallpox and diphtheria taking their toll, and it was a considerable achievement for the Jacksons to lose only one child at a relatively young age. Another

203	23	1	John Jackson	Head	Mar	45		Professional Cricketer	Notts	Nottingham	
			Mahalda do	Wife			43		[illegible]	[illegible]	
			John Jackson	Son	Unm	19		Dock labourer	Notts	Retford	
			Kate do	Daur			16	Shop Assistant	do	do	
			Henry do	Son		15		[illegible]	do	do	
			Samuel do			11		Scholar	Lancashire	[illegible]	

1881 Census which gives Jackson's occupation as Professional Cricketer.

284 Beaufort Street

Mr Tinley
Sir
can you send me 15 pounds
as I want to sell Milk and
to buy a 2hand Cart and there
wants a many things to
begin with it as been
very Slack this Winter but
I hope it will soon be better
I have plenty of things in
the shop that is lying
ded
You can send Post
Office Order to be maid
payable at Park Place
let me hear from you
I remain yours respectfully
H Jackson

P.S have you Got all
the money in the

Letter from Jackson to Tinley asking for financial help.
This may have been written by Henry Jackson who is described in the 1871 census return as a milk deliver seller.

daughter, Lucie, had been born on 16 January 1875 at 8 Beaufort Street Liverpool, and she is listed as a scholar along with Samuel. The eldest three children were now working, John as a dock labourer, Kate as a shop assistant and Harry as a milk seller. And thereby hangs another of the little mysteries that keep intruding into this biography. In the early 1870s we find Jackson writing to his old pal, Richard Tinley, asking him for money, £15, to help him to buy a milk lorry. Jackson had begun to find himself in more straitened circumstances as the money he could earn from cricket dried up. It seems that Tinley may have sent the money as John Jackson is shown on Lucie's 1875 birth certificate as a 'provision dealer', although by 1881 he had reverted on the census to being a professional cricketer, the only job he had ever known. He may also have bought the lorry out of the proceeds of his benefit match, of which more anon. It is perhaps too simplistic to regard Tinley as a generous benefactor.

[Printed by authority of the Registrar General.]

CK 286568

B. Cert.
S.R.

CERTIFIED COPY of an ENTRY OF BIRTH
Pursuant to the Births and Deaths Registration Act 1953

Registration District West Derby & Toxteth Park

1875. Birth in the Sub-district of Toxteth Park in the County of Lancaster.

Columns:—	1	2	3	4	5	6	7	8	9	10*
No.	When and where born	Name, if any	Sex	Name, and surname of father	Name, surname and maiden surname of mother	Occupation of father	Signature, description, and residence of informant	When registered	Signature of registrar	Name entered after registration
120	Sixteenth January 1875 284 Beaufort Street	Lucy	Girl	John JACKSON	Elizabeth JACKSON formerly REVEL	Provision dealer	J. Jackson Father 284 Beaufort Street Toxteth Park.	Sixteenth February 1875	Thos Evans Registrar.	

*See note overleaf

Certified to be a true copy of an entry in a register in my custody.

Carole Codd Superintendent Registrar

12. 12. 1996. Date

CAUTION:—It is an offence to falsify a certificate or to make or knowingly use a false certificate or a copy of a false certificate intending it to be accepted as genuine to the prejudice of any person, or to possess a certificate knowing it to be false without lawful authority.

WARNING: THIS CERTIFICATE IS NOT EVIDENCE OF THE IDENTITY OF THE PERSON PRESENTING IT.

Lucy Jackson's birth certificate. She was Jackson's youngest daughter. Jackson is this time described as a provision dealer.

Over the last twenty years of his life things started to go steadily more pear-shaped for Jackson as he fell on hard times. We must appreciate that in those days there was no safety net for those who could not cope with life and its problems. There was no benefit system, no NHS, and the sole refuge offered was the Victorian workhouse. John Jackson only knew how to play cricket and, great player that he was, he had neither trained for anything else nor had he been fully educated. He did some jobs in the warehouses on the Liverpool docks, but this giant of a man who had once struck terror into the hearts of batsmen of international class and could keep going all day, was now competing for jobs with men who were considerably younger and fitter than he was. In 1882 he became a father again at the age of 49 when his youngest child, Harold, was born at 23 Carlton Hill on 15 August.

At some point over the next few years the family began to split up. In 1889 Kate was married to a glazier from Devon named Samuel Dovey from Nickelby Street, Liverpool, and by the 1891 census had set up home at 47 Ouse Street, Toxteth. Harry was also married to a lady from Worcester, named Esther. In 1891 they were living at 64 Greenbank Hall, Toxteth Park and had a baby daughter, Maud, aged two. Living with Samuel and Kate at 47 Ouse Street were their two children, Samuel H., aged one and Alfred, aged two months. Also living there were John Jackson's children, Samuel R. who was by now a postman's messenger, and Harold, as scholar, as well as Lucie who was still at school. But John and Mahala – where were they?

Mahala, sadly, was dead. She had been living at 8 Madryn Street, Toxteth. This was a terraced street about half a mile from Liverpool Cathedral. Recently much of the area was earmarked for development but it was discovered that No. 9 was one of the childhood homes of Ringo Starr of Beatles fame. It soon became a tourist attraction. She passed away of a pulmonary illness on 4 February 1891. Her son, Samuel R. was present at the death and signed the death certificate. John seems not to have been

CERTIFIED COPY OF AN ENTRY OF DEATH — GIVEN AT THE GENERAL REGISTER OFFICE

Application Number 1921384-1

REGISTRATION DISTRICT TOXTETH PARK

1891 DEATH in the Sub-district of Toxteth Park in the Counties of Liverpool and Lancaster

No.	When and where died	Name and surname	Sex	Age	Occupation	Cause of death	Signature, description and residence of informant	When registered	Signature of registrar
153	Fourth February 1891. 8 Madryn Street Liverpool. U.S.D.	Mahala Jackson	Female	52 years	Wife of John Jackson a Professional Cricketer	Phthisis Pulmonalis Certified by J. J. [illegible] M.R.C.S.	J. R. Jackson Son Present at the death 47 [illegible] Street Toxteth Park	Fifth February 1891	Wm Russell Deputy Registrar

CERTIFIED to be a true copy of an entry in the certified copy of a Register of Deaths in the District above mentioned.

Given at the GENERAL REGISTER OFFICE, under the Seal of the said Office, the 8th day of January 2010

DYC 560801

See note overleaf

CAUTION: THERE ARE OFFENCES RELATING TO FALSIFYING OR ALTERING A CERTIFICATE AND USING OR POSSESSING A FALSE CERTIFICATE ©CROWN COPYRIGHT

WARNING: A CERTIFICATE IS NOT EVIDENCE OF IDENTITY.

Mahala Jackson's 1891death certificate with Jackson described as a professional cricketer.

present, and there are good reasons to believe that the pair had gone their separate ways by then.

John is shown on the 1891 census as living at 4 Frederick Street, Liverpool 1, in the seedy Park Lane area of the city where brothels and cheap 'doss-houses' were the normal accommodation. John Jackson was by now on skid row, living in a common lodging-house with 14 other men of various ages and occupations, the oldest being 76 and the youngest 18. None are listed as 'retired'. John is shown as a 'cotton porter'. In those days you either worked until you dropped or you went in the workhouses, stigmatised as a failure.

John Scully	Do	S	21	Ships Cattle man	X	[illegible] Blackstone
Thomas Wright	Do	M	53	Ships Freight Clerk	X	Cornwall Truro
John Jackson	Do	Wd	58	Cotton Porter	X	Suffolk Bungay
John Oneill	Do	S	18	Dely Porter	X	L'pool

1891 Census. Jackson is now described as a cotton porter.

Quite how Jackson had come to fall so far is something of a mystery. We do know that he was not by any means the only professional cricketer to fall upon hard times after his career had finished. Indeed, Ted Pooley, the old Surrey and England wicketkeeper and a near contemporary with Jackson, also ended his days in poverty as a workhouse resident. Others, unable to cope with the loss of fame and the camaraderie of their fellow professionals, opted to take their own lives. Their moving stories are told by David Frith in his book, *By their own Hand.* Bobby Peel, the great Yorkshire

Madryn Street.

8 Madryn Street today.

bowler, was forced out of the game by drink, and it is more than possible that drink was a party to Jackson's demise also. After all, the All-England Cricketers spent so long away from home with fellow professionals and the inevitable 'hangers-on' for company, that many turned to drink, and there were always plenty of offers to feed their habit from members of the public keen to boast about taking liquid refreshment with a star cricketer of the AEE. Pullin in the course of his interview with Jackson mentions that the fast bowler 'had his demons' but does not elaborate further. Richard Daft mentions that 'Jackson was always getting into scrapes' but goes no further than that. There are some clear hints that there was in Jackson's makeup a flaw that was to cause his downfall.

So drink may have been a problem. So might his temper. We have noted how he regularly hurled down beamers at top pace at batsmen who defied him for long. We have noted that he was not above deliberately hurling a ball he had fielded to hit Carpenter in an AEE v UAE match, after that batsman had hit Jackson about a bit. Then there was his refusal of his captain's request to kiss a Maori lady in New Zealand. Were these symptoms of a malaise within Jackson which, coupled with a fondness for drink, made him a hard companion to live with when he was about all the time? After all, Mahala and the children had seen little of him when he was still playing cricket which had involved long absences from home.

No man could get rich playing cricket in the mid-nineteenth century. After his retirement from cricket Jackson's income would have dropped considerably. Nottinghamshire gave him a benefit in 1874 which raised £300, not a negligible amount for those days and one which should have helped help him through old age. The fact that it did not is perhaps some indication of the kind of life he led and the type of man he was. It is likely that Mahala and the children grew tired of having this morose, bad-tempered man living with them and the result was a split up serious enough to preclude him living with any of them.

Jackson had no trade to fall back on once his playing days were over. Nor had he received much, if anything, in the way of a formal education. Left on his own the only help that Jackson seems to have received on a regular basis in his later desperate years was a weekly payment of 5s 6d from the Cricketers' Benevolent Fund. He was also being helped by the Sugg brothers, Albert and Frank, ex-professional cricketers with Derbyshire and Lancashire and in the 1890s sports outfitters in Whitechapel, Liverpool. Hearing of Jackson's situation, they set him up in lodgings and did their best to care for him. Despite their best efforts, though, he did spend some time in the Liverpool Workhouse.

The Victorian Workhouse was a refuge of last resort. When you were down and out, sick or penniless the workhouse was the only place where you could go if you did not want to sleep in the street. A stigma was attached to the workhouse and families tended to be ashamed of relatives who finished up in one of them.

Jackson's last years were spent either in the workhouse on Brownlow Hill,

FUNERAL OF A FAMOUS OLD NOTTS CRICKETER.

The remains of John Jackson, the famous old Notts cricketer, who died on Monday last, at the Brownlow hill Infirmary, were interred yesterday afternoon at Smithdown-road Cemetery. The Rev Dr Hardern, chaplain to the Brownlow-hill Workhouse, officiated at the service prior to the interment and also at the graveside. The principal mourners were Mr and Mrs. S. R. Jackson (son and daughter-in-law), Messrs Harold and John Jackson (sons), Mrs. Dovey (daughter), and Mrs. H Jackson (daughter-in-law). Amongst those who assembled at the graveside to pay a last token of respect to the old cricketer were Messrs. Frank and Walter Sugg, A J Bailey, C Brewer, A G Gibson, J S. Huthersal, George Ubsdell, J Atkinson, J Pritchard, T. A Mather, W B Dumbell, and F P Moss. Wreaths were sent by the relations and Messrs. Frank and Walter Sugg. The arrangements were carried out by Messrs. W and D. Busby, Low hill. After the interment the Rev Dr Hardern, who, by the way, is also an old cricketer, gave a short address, in which he spoke in sympathetic terms of the prowess of the deceased as a cricketer. He had, said the speaker, played a great innings and had established a reputation of being one of the best bowlers of his time. A telegram regretting his inability to be present was received from Mr J W Denham, of Yorkshire County C C. The fund, which was opened by Mr Frank Sugg for the purpose of defraying the cost of the funeral, &c of John Jackson, the famous old Notts cricketer, has benefited by a couple of guineas from Messrs Alfred Robinson and Edward Hodgkinson, of Rotherham.

Liverpool Echo report of John Jackson's funeral.

Liverpool or in various cheap lodging houses in the Liverpool Docks area. On one occasion he was admitted to the workhouse after being found by a policeman collapsed in a shop doorway in Russia Street

In May 1901 Jackson was admitted to the Workhouse Infirmary after a fall in his lodgings at 31 Duke Street. Duke Street had declined from being a street where three Mayors of Liverpool had once lived along with leading merchants to somewhere that offered cheap lodgings to the poor and unemployed for just a few pence a night. He died there on 4 November 1901 of complications brought on by his fall.

He was buried in Toxteth Cemetery, Smithtown Road with the Rev'd W.Hardern, the Brownlow Hill Workhouse Chaplain, officiating at the service and the interment as well as giving the Address. Although Jackson had clearly died as a pauper, the funeral expenses were defrayed by a fund set up by the Suggs through the Liverpool papers and supported by many old cricketing friends which was well subscribed so this was not strictly a pauper's funeral. Jackson's son, Samuel, bought the plot where his father was buried and he was eventually to be buried in the same plot.

The inscription on John Jackson's grave in Toxteth Cemetery, Smithdown Road, Liverpool. [Nottinghamshire CCC]

It should be noted that Mahala is also interred at Toxteth Cemetery. She lies in a different plot so they were not re-united in death. Jackson's sons, Samuel, John and Harold were among the chief mourners as was Kate with her husband Samuel Dovey. Harry did not attend and neither did his now estranged wife, Lucie. She had married William George Collins in 1897 and she had now moved away from Liverpool. The Sugg brothers and a number of other cricketing acquaintances and friends were there to pay their last respects and remember the good times he had had.

Despite efforts by the Suggs no headstone was erected until 2009 when a number of relatives, unaware that they were descendants of a famous cricketer, began researching their family tree. They traced the grave and collected £1200 for a proper headstone which was dedicated on 7 September 2009.

John Jackson was undoubtedly one of the great mid-Victorian cricketers. He was a genuinely fast bowler and had he had the fast bowler's touch of nastiness which made him not bother too much about whether he got a batsman out bowled or retired hurt. He was one of the first names on the team sheet for any of the big matches - Gentlemen v Players, AEE XI v United England XI, North v South. Had Test matches been played in those days he would almost certainly have been England's opening bowler. Both R.D.Walker and W.Caffyn considered that Jackson was the most difficult fast bowler to face in their day. As we have seen he was the subject of a Punch cartoon - the only cricketer to find his way into the pages of Punch before the advent of W.G.Grace.

In Volume VIII of *Scores and Biographies* Haygarth reproduced a lengthy piece of verse about the members of the team which visited Australia in 1863/64. It had this to say about Jackson:

> Jackson comes next: the ball's his special care
> His pace is awful, and e'en those that dare
> To stand against him, and their wicket shield,
> Are to his trundling often made to yield:
> 'Tis said that when he's really on the spot,
> To play those breakbacks and those shooters hot,
> A Pilch, a Mynn, a Daft combined 'twould take
> His balls to conquer and his bowling break.

What must it have been like for a batsman representing one of the XXIIs to stand at the crease watching this big 6 feet 4 inch man - and nasty with it - pacing out his run prior to bowling a ball faster than anything seen since the AEE's last visit? Nor was Jackson too particular about where he did some damage. Listen to his part of his interview with Old Ebor in *Talks with Old England Cricketers.* Jackson agrees that that he never took all 10 wickets in an innings, but 'I took nine once and lamed John Wisden so that he could not bat so that was as good as all 10, wasn't it?' This was the Jackson philosophy writ large. That said, he took many, many wickets bowled, caught, lbw and otherwise legitimately dismissed at a pace described by Prowse as 'fearful'. None of which, sadly, equipped him for what would happen when he could play no longer.

Peter and Tony Collins, two of John Jackson's great-grandsons. [Nottinghamshire CCC]

Acknowledgements

The trigger for this book was an article which appeared in the *Liverpool Daily Post* on Monday 7 September 2009 about a headstone to a famous cricketer which had been erected to the memory of John Jackson in Smithdown Road Cemetery, Liverpool. Reading the article I realised what a fascinating story could be woven around the life of this great fast bowler and I set about finding some of the relatives mentioned in the paper.

Thus I came to talk to Raymond Summers, grandson of Jackson's son Harry, and Peter Collins who through his grandmother Lucie is a great-grandson of John Jackson. I spent a day with Peter and his charming wife Pat at their home near Ludlow when Peter has assembled photographs and memorabilia relating to his great-grandfather. I shall never forget their hospitality and kindness or Peter's generosity in allowing me to have and to use copies of family photographs as well as copies of articles on Jackson's career. This kick-started my quest to find out more about Jackson's life. A visit to Peter Wynne-Thomas in the Trent Bridge Library opened up new lines of enquiry. To all of them go my thanks.

I have used Arthur Haygarth's *Scores and Biographies* as my primary match source, supplemented by contemporary accounts culled from local newspapers. I acknowledge the help that I was most freely and generously given by the staff at the following libraries in tracing reports of matches that John Jackson had played at their local grounds:- Accrington, Ashton-under Lyne, Barnsley, Bath, Bishop's Stortford, Blackburn, Bolton, Bradford, Bristol, Bury St Edmunds, Burnley, Carlisle, Chatham, Darlington, Derby, Dewsbury, Dudley, Durham, Godalming, Harrogate, Hereford, Huddersfield, Hull, Kendal, Leamington Spa, Leeds, Lincoln, Liverpool, Macclesfield, Manchester, Mansfield, Melton Mowbray, Middlesbrough, Newport (Mon), Neath, Nottingham, Oakham, Oldham, Peterborough, Plymouth, Redditch, Redruth, Retford, Scarborough, Sheffield, Sleaford, Southampton, Stoke-on-Trent, Tavistock, Truro, Wakefield, Walsall and York. Scanning this list you can see how widely and extensively the All-England Eleven spread their net and it gives you some idea of the amount of travelling involved.

Others who have helped include Mrs Christine Watts from The Museum of Wigan Life for helping to interpret census returns relating to the Jackson family.

A word of thanks too to Newark Cricket Club where Jackson started his career for assistance with and confirmation of records and for providing a copy of the All England Eleven which hangs in their pavilion.

My thanks go to both David Jeater of the ACS for his unfailing encouragement and to Roger Moulton for his work as editor. Thanks to Ray Greenall and Chris Overson for proofreading and to all at City Press for their work.

Select Bibliography

Books

First-Class Match Scores - various editions, Cardiff, ACS
Lillywhite, Fred. *English Cricketers in Canada and United States in 1859.* Tadworth Press, 1980
Altham, H.S. *A History of Cricket.* George Allen & Unwin, 1962. Darf, 1989
Ashley-Cooper, F.S. *Nottinghamshire Cricket and Cricketers.* Henry B.Saxton, 1923
Barrett, Norman. *Daily Telegraph Chronicle of Cricket.* Guinea Press, 1994
Bowen, Rowland. Cricket: *A History of its Growth and Development throughout the World.* Eyre & Spottiswoode, 1970
Daft, Richard. *Kings of Cricket.* J.W.Arrowsmith, 1893
Frith, David. *The Trailblazers - First English Tour of Australia 1861-62.* Goostrey, 1999
Pullin, A.W. *Talks With Old England Cricketers.* W.Blackwood & Sons, 1900
West, G Derek. *The Elevens of England.* Darf, 1988
West, Derek. *Twelve Days of Grace* Darf, 1989.
Wynne-Thomas, Peter. *Nottinghamshire Cricketers 1821-1914.* 1971

Appendix

Career Statistics

First-Class Cricket: Batting and Fielding

		M	*I*	*NO*	*Runs*	*HS*	*Ave*	*100*	*50*	*Ct*
1855	Eng	1	2	0	8	8	4.00	-	-	1
1856	Eng	3	5	1	19	11	4.75	-	-	4
1857	Eng	12	22	5	86	16*	5.05	-	-	10
1858	Eng	12	21	3	228	45	12.66	-	-	12
1859	Eng	10	18	4	177	41	12.64	-	-	7
1860	Eng	13	22	4	154	29	8.55	-	-	14
1861	Eng	14	24	4	158	41	7.90	-	-	15
1862	Eng	14	21	6	362	59	24.13	-	1	15
1863	Eng	10	17	3	282	100	20.14	1	-	10
1863/64	Aus	1	2	0	24	12	12.00	-	-	0
1864	Eng	10	17	1	237	68*	14.81	-	2	6
1865	Eng	10	14	2	209	55	17.41	-	1	7
1866	Eng	4	5	0	28	24	5.60	-	-	4
1867	Eng	1	1	0	21	21	21.00	-	-	-
Total		***115***	***191***	***33***	***1993***	***100***	***12.61***	***1***	***4***	***105***

First-Class Cricket: Bowling

		O	*M*	*R*	*W*	*BB*	*Ave*	*5i*	*10m*
1855	Eng	40	17	46	3	3/28	15.33	0	0
1856	Eng	43	16	70	10	4/?	14.00	0	0
1857	Eng	591.2	247	791	92	8/20	8.59	9	3
1858	Eng	706.1	260	1126	102	9/27	11.03	13	4
1859	Eng	696	281	919	83	8/32	11.07	9	4
1860	Eng	751	308	1003	109	9/34	9.20	11	5
1861	Eng	598.2	135	1094	81	7/31	13.50	9	2
1862	Eng	502.1	200	750	48	4/42	15.62	0	0
1863	Eng	470.3	202	666	58	7/48	11.48	5	2
1863/64	Aus	64	34	77	3	2/60	25.66	0	0
1864	Eng	299	126	377	22	3/17	17.13	0	0
1865	Eng	276.1	124	340	29	7/25	11.72	2	0
1866	Eng	85.1	31	137	8	4/18	17.12	0	0
1867	Eng	78.1	37	95	7	6/50	11.43	1	0
Totals		**5207**	**2018**	**7491**	**655**	**9/27**	**11.43**	**59**	**20**

First-Class Cricket: Five or more wickets in an innings (59)

Analysis	*For*	*Opponent*	*Venue*	*Season*
25.3-11-31-6	AEE	UAEE	Lord's	1857
41-18-53-8	North	South	Lord's	1857
32-15-38-7	North	South	Lord's	1857
35.3-69-7	England	Surrey&Sussex	Oval	1857
55-19-79-6	England	Surrey&Sussex	Oval	1857
38.1-16-45-8	England	Surrey&Sussex	Hove	1857
14-7-24-6	North	South	Tunbridge Wells	1857
13.2-6-18-7	North	South	Tunbridge Wells	1857
21-10-20-8	North	South	Trent Bridge	1857
36-13-50-5	AEE	UAEE	Lord's	1858
42-9-97-5	Notts	Surrey	Oval	1858
38-14-55-6	Players	Gentlemen	Oval	1858
25-14-27-9	Kent	England	Lord's	1858
28-8-37-6	North	South	Lord's	1858
13-5-19-5	Players	Gentlemen	Lord's	1858
34-14-40-6	AEE	UAEE	Lord's	1858
25.3-11-28-6	AEE	UAEE	Lord's	1858
34-12-58-5	North	Surrey	Oval	1858
44.3-23-62-7	Married	Single	Oval	1858
28-10-35-9	Kent	England	Canterbury	1858
34-14-54-5	Notts	Yorks/Durham	Stockton	1858
46.2-25-32-8	AEE	UAEE	Lord's	1859
39-20-29-6	AEE	UAEE	Lord's	1859
31-9-45-5	Players	Gentlemen	Oval	1859
15-6-21-6	England	Surrey	Oval	1859
52.3-20-71-6	North	Surrey	Oval	1859
16.1-8-21-7	North	South	Canterbury	1859
42-20-53-5	North	South	Canterbury	1859
48-18-71-6	North	Surrey	Broughton	1859
41.3-13-54-5	North	Surrey	Broughton	1859
18-6-19-5	England to USA	Another England XI	Old Trafford	1860
20.2-5-38-6	England to USA	Another England XI	Old Trafford	1860
18.1-6-24-6	Notts	Surrey	Oval	1860
35-14-49-9	Notts	Surrey	Oval	1860
40-23-40-7	AEE	UAEE	Oval	1860
41.1-16-62-8	England 1st XI	England Next XV	Lord's	1860
53-19-78-5	Notts	Surrey	Trent Bridge	1860
34-19-34-9	England	Kent	Canterbury	1860
37-19-54-8	North	Surrey	Broughton	1860
38-17-46-5	North	Surrey	Broughton	1860
20-11-24-5	North	South	Sleaford	1860
24.2-12-31-7	AEE	UAEE	Lord's	1861
31-8-77-5	Notts	Surrey	Oval	1861
17-0-31-6	Players	Gentlemen	Lord's	1861
31.3-0-68-5	Players	Gentlemen	Lord's	1861
25-4-64-5	AEE	UAEE	Old Trafford	1861
19-9-18-6	England	Kent	Canterbury	1861
36-15-51-7	North	Surrey	Broughton	1861
31.1-?-43-6	North	South	Aston Park	1861
27-?-43-5	North	South	Aston Park	1861
25-6-48-7	AEE	UAEE	Lord's	1863
20-10-41-5	Players	Gentlemen	Lord's	1863
29.3-18-23-6	Notts	Kent	Cranbrook	1863
34-22-20-6	Notts	Kent	Cranbrook	1863
37-20-34-6	North	South	Wavertree	1863
30.3-19-25-7	Notts	Surrey	Trent Bridge	1865
21-8-38-6	Notts	Cambridgeshire	Old Trafford	1865
42.1-22-50-6	AEE	UAEE	Lord's	1867

Jackson performed this feat 18 time at Lord's, 13 at The Oval, 5 times at Old Trafford, Canterbury and Broughton, three times at Trent Bridge, twice each at Cranbrook, Aston Park and Tunbridge Wells and once each at Hove, Stockton-on-Tees, Wavertree and Sleaford. In all matches at Lord's he took 206 wickets at 10.14 and at The Oval he took 160 at 15.33.He took 198 wickets for North of England teams, 140 for Nottinghamshire and 110 for the All-England Eleven.

Index

A page number in **bold type** indicates an illustration.